ARK ROYAL

Ark Royal

Kenneth Poolman

NEW ENGLISH LIBRARY
TIMES MIRROR

First published in Great Britain by Wm. Kimber & Co. Ltd., 1956
© William Kimber & Co., Ltd., 1956

*

FIRST NEL PAPERBACK EDITION JUNE 1974

*

NEL Books are published by
New English Library Limited from Barnard's Inn, Holborn, London, E.C.I.
Made and printed in Great Britain by Hunt Barnard Printing Ltd., Aylesbury, Bucks.

45001803 2

ACKNOWLEDGEMENTS

I WISH sincerely to thank all those ex-members of the old
Ark Royal's ship's company who have given me so much
kind help in the preparation of this book, especially
Rear-Admiral L. E. H. Maund, C.B.E., who was kind
enough to talk to me about the great ship he loved and
once commanded and to allow me to quote from his book
Assault from the Sea, Commander R. N. Everett, O.B.E.,
who gave me much of his valuable time and allowed me
to use some of his splendid photographs, Commander
R. E. Gardner, O.B.E., D.S.C., R.N.V.R., Commander
(E) A. G. Oliver, Lieutenant S. H. Leigh, M.B.E. and Mr
B. M. Seymour. I am also greatly indebted for much
interesting information to Mr J. Banks, Mr J. S. Bishop,
Mr J. H. Burnett, Mr C. D. Calder, Mr R. W. Christopher,
Mr A. Claydon, Mr J. Coward, Mr G. E. Denny, Captain
A. C. G. Ermen, A. D. C., Mr E. Eustance, Lieutenant
P. W. Hancock, B.E.M,, Mr E. W. J. Head, Mr G. P.
Hiscox, Mr R. Hornsby, Mr L. G. J. Howard, Mr L. H.
Kempshall, Mr K. J. Lord, Commander B. S. McEwan,
Mr G. C. O'Nion, Mr L. A. Pearson, Mr S. C. Tanner,

Mr S. Watson and Mr G. Wood.

My deepest thanks also go to Mr Reg Holmes, late of the Department of the Chief of Naval Information at the Admiralty, and now of Vickers Armstrong Ltd., to all the others in the Naval Information Department who have helped me so much, and to the Imperial War Museum. I also wish to acknowledge the invaluable general information derived from the books *Sea Warfare*, by Captain John Cresswell, R.N., *The War at Sea* 1939–1945, by Captain S. W. Roskill, D.S.C., R.N., and from Sir Winston Churchill's War Memoirs.

KENNETH POOLMAN.

CONTENTS

CHAPTER I

COME AND JOIN US!

IF ever there was a happy band of brothers it was the old Fleet Air Arm.

In theory this harmony looked impossible. The Fleet Air Arm was a hybrid force, part Royal Navy, part Royal Air Force. The R.A.F. legally owned it because it was, like Coastal Command, run by them, and mostly manned by them as well. The Royal Navy supplied the observers and some of the pilots and the Air Force the rest, including all maintenance personnel. Since all the aircraft were borne in their ships, however, the Fleet Air Arm was under the operational control of the Admiralty.

The F.A.A. was started in 1924 and struggled on bravely for just over a decade, all the time suffering from being a poor relation. It was kept short of aircraft, and those it did get were usually far inferior to current land-based machines. It did not seem worthwhile to try to design fast fighters and bombers to work from the carriers, because few people believed in the carrier as an effective weapon.

The only men who did believe in it were the men who

made it work. They practised torpedo attacks and bombing runs against ships, and their fighters were active and enterprising. They *knew* they had a big future.

For a long time die-hard opinion said they had not. Old-fashioned admirals stated categorically that they would all be shot down by the anti-aircraft guns of the ships, although, of course, they ought to be carried with the fleet to scout for its big guns. The Fleet Air Arm enthusiasts in their turn thought they could supplement, even replace, the big guns and do a much better job.

Air Force bomber fanatics insisted that land-based bombers would blow any warship afloat to smithereens in a few minutes. Air Arm fighter pilots were invariably very rude when anybody put this forward as a serious idea. 'Give us fighters that can hold their own with the best land-based types,' they said, 'and we will make short work of your precious bombers!'

Everyone, from hard-working pilot to armchair air-marshal argued the point, but nobody really knew the answer.

It was impossible, short of a real war, to test the theories. But wise thought in both the Royal Navy and Royal Air Force could see from the daring and skilful work of 'The Branch' in that long, long, thankless decade in the wilderness that there was a definite place of importance for the aircraft that went down to the sea in ships.

That was why, in 1934, the Navy and the Air Force were fighting tooth and nail for the ownership of the Fleet Air Arm.

It was why the Admiralty decided in that year that they must build another aircraft carrier, and make it the very best ship of its kind in the world.

They suffered from two very great handicaps.

First, they did not have much money to spend. The Fleet had previously been 'cut to the bone', as the First Lord had said, and now, when Britain was beginning to see its folly in cutting any of its fighting forces down to such a perilously low state, the Treasury would vote it little enough with which to build the cruisers and destroyers which were its greatest need, let alone new aircraft carriers, which were ruinously expensive.

But they could squeeze out just enough for a limited addition to the six existing old carriers, most of which were makeshift jobs converted from battleships and heavy cruisers.

At this point they came up against the second, and greater obstacle, and 'My Lords' had to sit down again and do another sum.

By the Washington Naval Treaty Great Britain and the United States were only allowed a carrier tonnage of 135,000. In this year of 1934 Britain had six carriers: *Argus*, *Eagle*, *Hermes*, *Furious*, *Glorious*, and *Courageous*. Their total tonnage was roughly 115,000.

It was a simple bit of addition and subtraction, and the answer came to 20,000 tons. That was the figure admirals doodled on their blotters. Whatever carrier or carriers we built, we could not have more than that.

The only freedom of choice the Navy had was between one largish carrier and two small ones. They had their own ideas about that, and there were examples abroad to guide them, too.

The United States had started with monster carriers. At the time of the Washington Treaty in 1922 they had two big battlecruiser hulls on the stocks consigned to scrap. A clause was inserted in the Treaty which allowed them to turn these white elephants into carriers of 33,000 tons each, the *Lexington* and *Saratoga*. Then they did their simple arithmetic and decided to split the 69,000 tons left amongst five brand-new ships, each of 13,800 tons, Japan followed the trend with carriers of 7,000 and 10,000 tons.

But by 1934 the U.S. Navy had changed its idea of five small carriers to include three of 20,000 tons. 14,000 tons they now considered inadequate, and experience had shown that *Lexington* and *Saratoga* were too big.

11

The only new carrier Britain had built was the *Hermes*, and she was too small – a graceful little experiment.

'The *Hermes*,' said her designer, Sir Eustace d'Eyncourt, at a meeting of the Institute of Naval Architects, 'is the only British vessel that has hitherto been designed from the start expressly as an aircraft carrier.

'In this case I was instructed to combine, in as small and economic a ship as possible, all the requirements of an efficient aircraft carrier, and the *Hermes*, of 10,000 tons, with a length of six hundred feet, was the result.

'Although she proved to be an efficient aircraft carrier, yet she suffered from the disadvantage of not having the length and size of the larger ships, and I am personally of the opinion that a bigger vessel, of a length not less than six hundred and fifty to seven hundred feet, should be aimed at.

'The bigger ship certainly makes a steadier platform than the smaller one, and the pitching in the larger ships is of less amplitude and less angle than in the shorter vessel, and this helps the operation of flying on and off. . . . '

That was current Admiralty opinion in 1934, and as a result the Board of Admiralty outlined preliminary staff requirements for one new carrier of about 20,000 tons. They wanted a clean, fast ship that would carry enough aircraft to make her pay and embody all the latest ideas, so that she would be able to cope with the new, fast aircraft that were being talked about.

They wanted a new super-carrier to take to sea the new exclusively naval air branch when the enthusiasts who were now lobbying their cause so relentlessly had brought off this long-desired coup.

Their first demands were out of the question. They asked for a flight-deck of nine hundred feet, and the naval constructors told them that such a length was impossible within the limitations of 20,000 tons. But if the Board agreed to reducing the length by a hundred feet they thought they could plan a light hull to carry it and still give the necessary stability and performance by making the flight-deck itself overhang the hull. With the restriction imposed upon them by the Treaty regulations their solution would not be the ideal one but it would be a very good compromise.

The final sketch design received Board of Admiralty approval on 21st June 1934. On paper she looked good.

Three screws giving 32,000 horsepower on each shaft would drive her at thirty knots and make sure that there would always be enough wind down that long, flush, eight-hundred-foot deck to get her aircraft airborne as well as take her out of harm's way when enemy big guns were in the vicinity. For she was not meant for gun duels. Her guns were to keep off enemy bombers, and her attacking power lay in her aircraft.

She would carry seventy-two of these, bombers and fighters, in two big hangars, one on top of the other, and one hundred thousand gallons of petrol deep down in her hull to keep them flying. Flight-deck arrangements would be of the very latest kind.

They gave the job, along with a three-million-pound contract to Cammell Laird's of Birkenhead.

Merseyside heard the news with thankfulness. Hundreds of good men who had been on the dole for years would be able to work again. It was the longest ship ever built on the river and the fattest contract the Admiralty had given out since the Great War.

So the new ship was a precious gift to us all. In return, her builders put every scrap of energy and expertise at their command into her. Her hull was welded instead of being riveted and much was made of the fact that she was the biggest ship built for the Royal Navy to be so constructed. In theory the saving in tonnage of a weight equivalent to the ship's entire gun armament by this method looked like a stroke of genius. Some people thought it was taking a big risk, however. The science of welding ships' hulls was in its infancy, and the hull of a great carrier like this one would have to withstand greater and more continuous strain than any other type of vessel. There were whispers of jerry-building, which was a fashionable expression at the time. But it was easy to throw stones. Stucco pretentiousness or daring modernity, ugly duckling or cygnet, it was for the future to decide.

Her launch was all wrong, and for an *ordinary* ship would have been ominous.

She went down the slipway on the 13th April 1937, after Lady Maude Hoare, wife of the First Lord, Sir Samuel Hoare, had made three futile attempts to smash the bottle of lucky champagne against those looming, lowering bows.

She was lucky the fourth time. The bottle shattered, there was a white thirsty splash like a snowball exploding, and Lady Hoare said, with great relief,

'I name this ship *Ark Royal*. May God guide her and guard and keep all who sail in her!'

Ark Royal. This ship was setting her sights high. The Navy obviously meant her to do great things, with such a name. It made you think at once of the Armada, when a small band of British seamen had broken the heart of Spain, and an *Ark Royal*, wearing the flag of Lord Howard of Effingham, had led the van. The motto of that old flagship was 'Désir n'a répos' ('Purpose knows no rest'), and she had passed it on, through three other proud ships of the name, to this strange, ugly-lovely lady. She took to the waters like a queen and seemed to carry her great inheritance and wear her titles with casual ease, bred to the purple.

Then she was towed along to her fitting-out berth to have her mighty engines lifted into her and all her intricate, intimate fittings and appointments – the most elegant ever built into a ship of war – grafted on to the bare steel bones. For she was really only a flat-topped hulk yet, hollow and rough hewn – a huge chrysalis with great hawse-holes like eyes, and protruding antennae where her aircraft catapults would be.

But when the first men of her ship's company saw her she had more identity, for by then the landmark of her bridge-island structure was up on the starboard side. Her big, flat-sided funnel was part of the Birkenhead scene by now, telling a landman which sharp end was which.

It was a very little structure, one of her new officers mused, to house the brain of a mighty ship; not in the least like a battleship's cluttered pagoda of flag-decks and admiral's bridges and bulbous fire-control platforms. It was little more than a flying bridge, really, perched precariously on the edge of the eight-hundred-foot sea-borne airstrip of grey steel.

Ark Royal's new Commander (Air) was one of the first to arrive. He would have his headquarters on the bridge island. From his flying-control position there he would be able to watch and manipulate all flying operations below him on the flight-deck. When he first saw his new place of business he eyed her very critically.

She looked a bit of a hybrid to anybody examining her long, straight shape. She had the same boxed-in look as the *Argus*, the same single funnel to starboard as the *Glorious* and *Courageous*. But her flight-deck, carried right up to the bows, was obviously a vast improvement. And the bows themselves were carried right up into the for'ard end of the flight-deck, which gave her a much more streamlined look than any of the old carriers had.

Other features caught the eye as well. If someone had asked the gunnery officer for his impressions he might have said that he rather liked her armament – sixteen of the new 4.5-inch guns, four pom-poms, and eight multiple machine-guns – and especially the way in which the guns had been mounted high up round the edge of the flight-deck. This was a great advance on the other carriers, whose guns were mostly placed so low that they gave a badly restricted arc of fire.

The executive commander liked that, too. It made it so much easier for boats to come alongside and saved a lot of wear and tear on his precious paintwork. But it remained to be seen how that big, sheer-sided hull would handle at sea in a wind. Carriers were notoriously clumsy in a wind, like floating haystacks, although here again *Ark Royal* presented a much lower silhouette than the others.

One by one, all the new heads of departments came up to Birkenhead to stand by the ship and work alongside the builders' men in the fitting out of their respective branches. Each department head had his assistant, so there were eleven officers in that first batch of key men and eleven ratings.

One of the assistants found himself the boss. Chief Petty Officer Sam Leigh came up from Portsmouth to be number one to Commander Hawkesworth, the ship's paymaster commander, a very important figure indeed in the fitting-out process, for he was the man responsible for all stores and supplies, other than gunnery stores, not to mention all matters of victualling and pay. But Commander Hawkesworth was on leave in Ireland when Sam joined, and fitting-out was a closed book for him, for he had never commissioned a new ship before, let alone a great new aircraft carrier.

He had to draw heavily upon his fifteen years' experience of the supply branch to do battle with this enormous task. The paymaster commander had over a hundred compartments in his charge.

Sam had seen a bit of domestic naval history in his time. The old Navy had never bothered much about its housekeeping. A ship's stores were left in charge of the departmental officers concerned, who rarely had a head for balancing the books. Stocks were not regulated at all and replenishments made whether they were actually needed or not.

The Great War with its vast fleets and prodigious logistic requirements showed up this archaic muddle for what it was, and shortly afterwards the old order changed. All stores were brought within the control of the paymaster and a new branch, the supply branch, was formed to work the new system.

Sam was one of its founder members. He went, as a brand-new supply assistant, to the *Courageous* before her conversion into a carrier, when she was a pretty ship, one of Jackie Fisher's lightweight battlecruisers. This was in the days of the daily 'standard ration' – half a pound of meat, a pound of potatoes, three-quarters of an ounce of milk, two ounces of sugar, one ounce of jam, a quarter-ounce of tea, two ounces of bread, and a quarter-pound of corned beef or salmon weekly as supper ration. The messing allowance then was sevenpence a day – but you could get a pound of beef or mutton for fourpence half-penny! Butter, bacon, and margarine, however, were not to be had. They did not figure on a sailor's shopping list until after 1937, and the *Ark Royal* just came in for them.

One of the first things Sam did after his first visit to the ship was to get a torch, and most of the others had to do the same. The ship was dark and huge inside, full of vast hollow places that seemed to bear no resemblance whatsoever to the inside of a ship. Strange mystic numbers chalked on bulkheads were the only means of finding your way about, and the thousands of tangled, wandering leads and the rough wooden ladders everywhere made you wonder if she would ever become ship-shape.

So it was with some relief that this handful of men, the pioneers, watched the dockyard slowly draw astern when *Ark Royal* raised steam for the first time and headed for the open sea.

There were some teething troubles. The forty-foot overhang of the flight-deck astern and the position of the rudder immediately abaft the centre screw put an unusual strain upon her lightly built structure aft, and it was necessary to stiffen some of the lighter plating.

Then it was found that smoke tended to drift down from the funnel and obscure the landing-on area. The funnel was raised eight feet and the trouble appeared to vanish. Then the rudder jammed at speed and she had to go back to the Mersey for docking and alterations.

There were more trials in the Clyde in July, followed by the final fitting-out. Sam Leigh and others took the opportunity of going to see the Bellahouston Exhibition in Glasgow.

Sam's duties were now concentrated on commissioning, making ready to receive the draft which was to arrive from Portsmouth ready to take the ship over from the dockyard men when they finally handed her over to the Navy. He had to prepare demands for provisions, clothing, mess traps and equipment for the galley. It was a big house to get ready for the new tenants.

For the latter, coming up from Pompey was like a mass evacuation. What a conglomeration of bags and baggage! It needed four trucks to take the gear alone. They were mustered and checked and marched and detailed off for what seemed like an age. Finally, clutching the usual wretched little bag meal, they were off in the special train.

The journey north took all day and they felt stale and filthy and fed up when they arrived at Liverpool in the evening. But they still had to hump all that baggage on to the transport. When they had done that they were just about ready to kip down where they stood. They were fallen-in again then and marched in a long column of rather ragged fours through the streets of Birkenhead to the shipyard. The people of the town were not used to the sight of so many men in blue together and they attracted a lot of attention, especially from the girls.

They could see the ship long before they got to the dockyard gates. Up there in the dusk she towered, a heavy, sombre shape against the gloom of the night. It was somehow a menacing, a foreboding sight to a lot of tired and browned-off matelots.

This impression deepened as they got nearer and the ship grew even bigger, towering above everything, dwarfing the docks themselves. By her looming, dark side they were halted and turned into line. Tired out, dirty, un-shaven, and uneasy as only men lost in the limbo of the draft can be, they stood and stared fixedly at *Ark Royal*'s great flanks. She looked like a tomb. Then they began to file aboard.

It was like waking in a feather bed. The 'tomb' was warm and bright with light and welcome. It was all big and friendly and wonderful, comfort personified. It was home.

How spick and span she was! How beautifully clean and bright! There was gleaming new mess gear, spotless tables and rubber-covered mess stools, and heaters on the messdeck to keep the food warm.

Here there were plenty of washbasins, and water that was always hot in a big modern bathroom equipped with showers. There was a greatcoat room, a big recreation space with a giant 'uckers' board marked out on the deck, and a barber's shop run by the Naafi. These were all startling innovations. Even the tallest matelot could hold his head up in this ship, where there was, for once, adequate deckhead clearance above it. It was love at first sight for them all.

Was there ever a time, Leading-Seaman Cyril Calder asked himself wonderingly, when he had sworn there could never be another ship like his beloved *Ajax*? He had been with that lovely ship throughout her first com-mission on the West Indies station.

Calder had seen his own footprints on the beach where Robinson Crusoe saw Man Friday's – barren Juan Fernandez, Alexander Selkirk's lonely kingdom three hundred miles off the west coast of Patagonia, visited now only by the savage winds that blow there. Then, heading south again and round the grey hell of Cape Horn, he had been to the icy prairies of South Georgia seas where whales roamed like buffalo herds in the blue deeps, and on to Port Stanley in the Falklands to see Ernest Shackle-ton's grave.

When the Antarctic summer declined they would cruise

north again. Passing Montevideo and the Plate it would have been hard to imagine that *Ajax* would ever fight a great battle in those lazy waters. . . .

Rio was all warmth, all rum and rumbas after bleak Patagonia and the white desolation south of forty. *Ajax*'s trojans always had a welcome there, especially the ship's harmonica band, Cyril among them. The band broadcast in Rio and appeared in cabaret, and the Latins were wild about them.

And the spirit in *Ajax* was magnificent. They all loved her and swore by her.

Now it looked as if he would have to undo that oath, thought Cyril grudgingly, now he had seen the *Ark*. . . .

You could say the same thing for Jack Bishop, able seaman and expert in ordnance. He had been serving in destroyers, battleships and cruisers, from the little *Velox* to the beautiful, tragic *Hood*, mint of so many fine sea-men-gunners, and he knew a happy ship when he saw one.

The whole commission started especially happily for him because his own eldest son, young Jack, joined the ship with him as a Royal Marine drummer-boy. So the Bishops went two by two into the *Ark*, not to get out of the rain, but to join another happy family.

Jack was Guns – A.B. Qualified Ordnance. He assisted the ordnance artificers in the care and maintenance of the armament, and worked as a seaman as well. That meant that he was always busy.

Chief Petty Officer Cook Vatcher, key man if ever there was one, prepared to feed sixteen hundred men. In this ship he had the very latest kind of galley to work in, with serving-hatches and washing-machines. Christmas was coming now and the geese were getting fat. Chiefie made the best Christmas puddings in the Navy.

The new men slept a sleep of exhaustion and happy relief that night. Next morning they went to sea for final acceptance trials, and on their successful completion the captain took over the ship on behalf of the Navy.

About three hundred of the firm's men had been embarked for the trials, and after the handing-over the ship returned to Liverpool Bay to transfer them ashore in tugs.

Then fog closed in upon them and they could not leave the ship. It looked as if they would have to spend the night at sea. Sam Leigh was told to issue three hundred extra lots of bedding. But just before midnight the fog cleared and the men departed – leaving their borrowed bedding scattered about the ship for Sam and his men to collect.

Then the pioneers pitched in with a will and took the ship to Portsmouth, her depot.

There she lay, grey and mighty, at Asia Pontoon on Boxing Day, 1938, a huge ugly duckling in a nest of war vessels. She was unfledged, unweathered yet, as anyone strolling through Portsmouth Dockyard on that raw winter's day could have seen. The Pompey landscape of jetties and sheds, tall masts and taller cranes poised like grey vultures against the pallid skyline, had not assimilated her, as it had the slimmer orthodoxy of battleships, cruisers, and destroyers. She was a stranger there, a young, sightless giant, a country cousin, gawky, gauche and awkward in the midst of her sophisticated sisters.

To the onlooker, the newness and strangeness of her would be his first impression. He would almost certainly be compelled to deny her beauty in the classical sense of the word, unless he were a Branch type. But majesty he could not deny her, majesty and immense dormant power, as in a great sleeping beast of prey.

But there wasn't a solitary onlooker on this cold grey day, and the ship was almost as empty as the dockside. In houses all over Portsmouth, and farther afield throughout Britain, the ship's company of H.M.S. *Ark Royal* lay comatose, full of every brand of Christmas spirit, with the exciting thought of their new ship and all she had already come to stand for to warm the cockles of their hearts still further. The few who had stayed aboard were falling-in blearily for part of ship, still vaguely fat and happy on

Andrew Miller's turkey and pusser's duff, or resting their outraged livers in the comfort of the elegant new wardroom, or in the home-from-home of a near-luxury cabin appointed as never before with the best that the taxpayers' money could buy and the naval contractors could fit.

Wherever you were spending your Christmas it was certainly much too cold and miserable to mooch around the dockyard or mess about in boats. Only the motorboat's duty crew had to worry about that – and they shouldn't have joined if they couldn't take a joke.

In fact they were the only ones out and about this morning. The little pinnace pushed a white bow-wave before her as she chugged across the cheerless harbour, half-way between the long, lovely, raking shape of the cruiser *Hawkins* and the Railway Jetty, just astern of *Ark Royal*.

'Shave off!' thought the cox'n, the stoker, and the wet and scowling bowman. 'All for one bloke! Boy seamen? I've spit 'em!' They did not look at the great *Ark* lying there in all her power and strength, only at the rosy mirage of tot-time.

But the boy seaman, their passenger, did. Clutching the new brass lock on the top of his kitbag, the shining pusser's boot resting on the sausage-like, drooping shape of his hammock, he stared for all he was worth, shivering with a mixture of cold and apprehension.

New office-boy and trembling apprentice have their moments of agony on that awful first day, but for this matelot about to join his first ship it was worse – more like the feelings of a raw powder-boy flung for the first time on to the airless gun-decks of Nelson's *Victory*.

The only Royal Navy he had known so far was H.M.S. *Ganges*, the training depot at Shotley, near Ipswich. He was very glad to have left *Ganges* behind, the 'stone frigate' that was sometimes concentration camp, institution, and penitentiary rolled into one to him, where 'Searchlight' and 'Creeping Jesus', the Marine, stalked the decks. There was only one relief for him at *Ganges*. The towering mast on the parade ground, a terror to most, was his sanctuary. He had seen one boy, in his misery, throw himself from the yard and crash to his death below, but he himself actually revelled in climbing it, especially the dreaded 'elbow', where the climber had to leave the main ratlines and climb outwards on his back like a fly until he had reached the edge of the cross-trees and swarmed up over the edge. Up here above the main-topsail yard, thick as an oak tree, which once had swung in wild parabolas above gale-ravaged seas, where the wooden ships and iron men of the old Royal Navy had kept station, up here he was immune for a brief moment. Here he could cling in his loneliness and dream of foreign lands and happy sailors lying under white canvas in the sun.

That was *Ganges*. Now it was *Ark Royal*.

'It'll be like going from one Alcatraz to another,' he thought.

The carrier had no sea-gangway down, so they landed him at Dockyard Steps on Railway Jetty, astern of her, and he walked along to the gangway from there, dragging bag and hammock and attaché case with him.

His eyes could not take in enough of her. When he stood for a moment and looked up at the immense curved overhang of the flight-deck aft he could not believe it. She was so huge, and her sides were like cliffs of steel, the flight-deck looming high above like a great gun-fringed plateau. He gaped in bewilderment at her great hull, stretching for what seemed like miles along the wire-festooned jetty, and wondered where in all that great shape was his messdeck, and whether there would be anyone he knew on board yet, any of the *Ganges* boys. The ship was lying, he noted, with her great bows to the open sea, and lighters lay clustered alongside her. He thought, *'I shall soon be going to sea in her for the first time.'* Until now his only sea-time had been a brief trip in an old destroyer just outside the breakwater.

The jetty was empty and deserted. A cold wind blew scraps of litter over the dirty stones. A paper streamer, fag end of Christmas and happy Noël, wrapped itself round a berthing-wire and streamed out stiff and absurdly proud in the breeze. The wind was cold, but it blew onshore and there was salt in it. Leaving his heavy kit-bag on the jetty, he slung his hammock over his shoulder, took a firm grip on his attaché case, and set his foot on the broad, steep, double gangway which rose majestically from the jetty and ended in a cavernous, gaping hole in the side of the *Ark*, big as the jaw that swallowed Jonah. The young matelot went up and was swallowed up, too, into the belly of this great leviathan that could gulp sixteen hundred men and sixty aeroplanes – and still be huge and honeycombed and vast.

There was a marine on the gangway, and a whole platoon of officers and men, it seemed. Nervously the young seaman handed in his joining slip, then doubled back down the gangway to fetch his kitbag, fearful of leaving any of that precious sea kit unattended. Then he was told to go through endless, echoing steel corridors and over high doorway bulkheads that barked your shins if you didn't look out, past strange, machinery-filled spaces dimly lit and humming, until he had found in the midst of all this man-made wilderness the fearful lair of the mighty master-at-arms.

The M.A.A. gave him a good chalking-off for calling him a petty officer, and Ron stood, numb and awestruck with it all, certain that he would never, never be able to find his way about this giant steel hive smelling strangely of oil and steam blended together into the unmistakable smell which all ships have. If someone had told him then that a few months later in a more urgent situation he would be able to get from the bridge to the lower conning-tower in thirty seconds, he would never have believed them.

But he found his mess at long last and made tentative efforts at settling in. He thoroughly approved of the big shining locker he was allotted to hold his gear. It was a custom of the lower-deck that a man left his relief a ten-shilling note in his locker for a run ashore, knowing that the new man has probably had nothing better than a 'casual' for some time. But there was no ten-bob note in his locker, and not a speck of dust either. For no one had ever had this locker before. He was the very first man to put his gear inside it. It gave him a queer sort of thrill.

He found there were ten other boys, all from the *Courageous*, on board, and he hung on their every word. After all, they were real veterans, real matelots with sea-time in an aircraft carrier. When he had unpacked his kit and stowed it away he slung his hammock ready for a much-needed kip and sat down to write a long letter home. This time, unlike *Ganges* days, he did not have to screen his experiences, but poured out all his young eager feelings about the ship, *his* ship, in whose life he, a boy seaman of fifteen, was to play a part, and about his hopes for the future, so bright now, so full of promise. . . .

CHAPTER II

PURPOSE KNOWS NO REST

LIEUTENANT-COMMANDER ERMAN was the first pilot to fly aboard H.M.S. *Ark Royal*. Behind him came the other Swordfish aircraft of his squadron, No. 820 Royal Navy. They were a crack squadron, and their speciality was flying from a carrier at night. They were a tough, thrusting crowd.

They came from the *Courageous*, which was giving her air group to the new ship. *Courageous* was not the easiest carrier in the world to work from. A pilot making his approach had to do a 'roundown creep' or else the air-flow over the stern might come at him like a waterfall and the hot gases from the funnel whisk him up just when he wanted to sink down. *Hermes*, built for the job, was an easier proposition. So was the *Furious*. She had no island, and the funnel gases, which were vented from pipes below the level of the flight-deck, did not bother a pilot as long as he came down the middle of the deck.

On 12th January 1939, aircraft of the Fleet Air Arm landed aboard their new carrier for the first time.

It was easy. No funnel gases here – that extra eight

feet added to the funnel during trials had worked. No roundown creep. They came straight on in and rolled up *Ark*'s enormous deck. But they had to do everything on the double. The Commander (Air) demanded landings at thirty-second intervals. When a pilot got down he was hustled below on the new electric lifts – much faster than on the old *Courageous* – into an enormous hangar, brilliantly lit. And the cabins! With tip-up beds and chromium plate everywhere instead of brass, they were the answer to a marine servant's prayer. Best mahogany everywhere; built-in settees and stainless-steel hot- and cold-water basins! A lieutenant's cabin was far better than a senior officer would have had in any of the old ships. As for the admiral's cabin, that was like a Hollywood film star's, with plastic panels and a sunk bath.

Of course the sheer size and complexity of everything was hard to get used to. There seemed to be vast numbers of officers everywhere, and at least three officers of the watch at a time. The captain was a tremendous personality and a great sailor. Nothing got by him, he was everywhere. He had the ship in the palm of his hand.

The commander was cast in the same mould. 'Big Bill' Eccles, six feet two, owner of the Japanese Black Belt for ju-jitsu, always seemed to be looking for an excuse to take off his coat, roll up his sleeves, and do somebody else's job as well as his own. They were two of a kind, Big Bill and the captain.

The Admiralty knew his worth when they appointed Captain Power to *Ark Royal* in command. He was a gunnery expert and had been captain of H.M.S. *Excellent*, the Royal Navy's secretly beloved Alcatraz, the place where ordinary men are turned into good Royal Naval gunners. He stood for discipline and relentless efficiency, and for the men he meant fair treatment. Some of the pilots got the feeling that he did not approve of his long-haired young chauffeurs, but saw them as a bunch of awkward, temperamental and irresponsible schoolboys who needed keeping in order.

He was a hard man and he had to be. For he was the bedrock upon which the efficiency and strength of this great new ship could alone be built. In the life of any ship her captain moulds her character. *Ark Royal* was not only brand new, she was unique. As a fighting ship she was big, awkward, and highly individual, and she needed a fine seaman to manage her. Furthermore, her hangars were full of aeroplanes, clumsy, smelly things when not in the air, and always a constant hazard to the ship, with their huge tanks of oil and aviation spirit buried deep in her bowels, and their big fire risk. Aeroplanes, of course, meant flying types, both R.N. and R.A.F.; the death-or-glory, harum-scarum fly boys who were always being rude about the 'fish-heads' who had no wings on their tunics, and battleship salthorses who could not see that the carriers were the capital ships of the future.

They might well be right. However, there was still a big place for guns, and the fanaticism of these young men had to be kept firmly in check. For they were on the crest of the wave. Only two years before, in the summer of 1937, Mr Chamberlain had said in the House:

'The proposals which the Government have had under their consideration refer to two classes of aircraft. The first class includes all aircraft borne in ships of the Royal Navy. These are known as the Fleet Air Arm. They are under the operational control of the Admiralty, but as part of the Royal Air Force they are under the administrative control of the Air Ministry. . . .

'In the case of the Fleet Air Arm the Government consider that these ship-borne aircraft should be placed under the administrative control of the Admiralty.'

It was great news for the pilots, observers and telegraphist-air-gunners of the Royal Navy. And now came the *Ark Royal*, first carrier of the new Fleet Air Arm, a test case for naval aviation, the anvil upon which the new branch could be hammered into shape or broken.

No wonder the Admiralty chose a man like Captain

Power to command her. No wonder they only picked the best men to run her, men who had on their records names like *Hood*, *Royal Sovereign*, *Ajax*, *Effingham*, *Iron Duke*, *Courageous*, *Warspite*, and *Queen Elizabeth*. They all felt that they were now serving in the finest ship afloat and that great things were expected of them. The men were happy under capable, fair-minded officers who looked after their welfare. They were a team and a family at one and the same time. If a man pitched in and did his job he was accepted as a member of the family. If he did not – God help him, for neither the captain nor the commander nor anybody else aboard would!

Good living conditions meant good morale. From the *Ark*'s galleys came the best food in the Navy. Commander Hawkesworth, the paymaster, made the feeding of the ship's company his primary concern. Food was cooked by his orders at the last possible moment to make sure that it was fresh and tasty when it reached the mess tables, and he formed the habit of dropping in on the cooks in the galleys to keep them on their toes. The general mess menu for the day, prepared with the accent on a varied and well-balanced diet by Vatcher, the chef, and Sam Leigh, the senior petty officer for victualling duties, had to pass his expert scrutiny.

Quite a bit of this excellent food was wasted when the ship went to sea, for while working up with the fleet in the Atlantic south-west of Fastnet she met the worst gale of her whole career. Huge green seas smashed over the flight-deck. In the hangars double lashings had to be put on the aircraft, and the noise everywhere was tremendous. All the cabin doors had been designed on the sliding principle, which was an excellent idea, except that the doors ran athwartships, and crashed together every time the ship rolled, with a noise like thunder or gunfire.

The breaking seas did heavy damage on deck. Even the navigation boxes were smashed and joiner Sid Tanner had to rebuild them completely. Sid was officially attached to the Fleet Air Arm, but as he was the senior joiner he had to accept other duties. He was responsible for some additions and alterations to the ship's chapel and played the organ there as well. He also looked after the captain's and admiral's beautifully appointed quarters. Captain Power, he found, was meticulous in looking after his own quarters. That endeared him to a conscientious craftsman like Sid. He also took note of the fact that the captain read his Bible every day without fail.

Seeing these little personal traits of the man, Sid, like many others in the ship, began to realise that they had a great captain. 'He's the finest officer and the greatest gentleman I've ever served under,' said Sid. When he said that he was thinking back over the years that included H.M.S. *London* and the First Cruiser Squadron, H.M.S. *Excellent* at Whale Island and the *Valiant*, one of the happiest ships in the Navy, cock of the Mediterranean Fleet in all sports – cricket, swimming, hockey and sailing.

Captain Power cleared the lower-deck and told them that *his* ship, *Ark Royal*, was now the finest ship in the Royal Navy and must be first in everything. Whether in deck hockey, football or flying efficiency, the *Ark* must beat them all.

And he added an ominous note. He was convinced, he told them, that war was imminent and he was certainly going to do his part in seeing that the *Ark* would be fighting fit in the shortest possible time.

Sid Tanner, listening intently as they all were at that serious and stirring moment, felt that the captain was the man to do it. Looking around him, he sensed that everyone else felt the same. They all meant to back him up with everything they had, whatever happened.

Those who read the news knew how badly things were going in Europe, and as the year drew on they saw the headlines grow taller and blacker as Nazi Germany like a great octopus began to devour her neighbours one by one. The promise of Munich had faded and the future looked uglier than ever.

At such a time the Royal Navy was the strongest shield of freedom. The men of *Ark Royal* felt this to be true, each in his own way, and knowing how much depended on them, redoubled their efforts.

Working up started smoothly, although everyone had their troubles.

'Tankey' John Banks had trouble with the domestic water supply which he looked after. 'It's like a blooming detective story trying to trace all the different systems,' he said disgustedly. They went by colours – blue for fresh water, red for salt (in the firemain), yellow for airline, and so on. Even with the colours it was very tricky some-times, in all the maze of pipes, to keep track of one particular line. John used to prevail upon an oppo to listen in, two or three bulkheads away, while he himself tapped the pipe until the other stoker gave him the signal that it was the right one.

After two or three weeks he had managed to get the general hang of things – a painful process which gave him a very good idea of the sheer vastness of the *Ark*. But the new lady's plumbing had its little foibles. The automatic switch gear on the gravity tanks was not at all healthy. It was too new and not yet properly run in, and when it got too badly constipated Stoker Banks would be piped for by an angry officer wanting a bath or the duty chef with a meal to cook and no water or a purple chief stoker wanting a perm. Water, water everywhere . . .

Similar things happened all over the ship and were soon seen to. They were mere teething troubles. The ship's gunners practised their shooting against Queen Bee radio-controlled aircraft. The supply system at the guns was unique to those who had been used to manhandling shells. In the *Ark* the shells came up to the guns in an endless chain controlled by photo-electric cells, and were fused at the guns. Flying routine was going well, although there were one or two crashes. The seaboat's crew were mustered at the double then, although there was always a destroyer 'crash boat' to race to the spot and pick up pilots who had force-landed in the sea. Everybody off watch used to gather on the catwalks round the flight-deck and on the 'goofers' platform' on the bridge to watch the flying and take photographs.

The new Skuas were powerful beasts. Lieutenant McEwan, a flight commander in 803 Squadron, thought, 'My God, this *is* an old tank!' when he collected his L2873 from Blackburn's at Brough. He had come from the gentler biplane Ospreys and Nimrods, and this new, all metal monoplane dive-bomber with 'mod cons' like dive flaps, a two-pitch airscrew and a retracting under-carriage, was altogether bigger and more potent. But he was soon declaring that they had no vices at all.

After *Courageous* he found, like all the pilots, that life had to be lived much faster on the *Ark*, and flying drill was more complicated. She had more arrester wires, and a proper barrier which was designed to stop overshooting machines and keep a space clear for'ard for striking-down aircraft which had just landed-on, or for parking, or actually flying-off planes from the catapult while others were still landing-on over the stern. It was an advance on the old method of jostling round the stern and letting the bravest man make the first dart at the deck, but *Ark* had not yet gone the whole hog like the Americans, and there was no deck-landing control officer or 'batsman' at this stage. The first senior man down grabbed the bats and brought the others in when the big shutter behind the funnel had flashed yellow – all clear to land-on!

Their first port of call on the spring cruise was Gibraltar. The *Ark* blotted her copybook mildly by foul-ing a buoy in harbour there, but otherwise the passage through the Mediterranean was unreservedly pleasant and sunny, with every department learning more and more each day about the part they had to play in running and fighting the *Ark*. The Signals Branch, for example, besides their normal duties keeping a watch for visual signals, practised hard by carrying out communication exercises with passing merchant ships.

At Malta there was an exchange of visits with the *Glorious*. *Ark Royal* pilots were rude about the comparatively mean quarters which their opposite numbers had to suffer, while Captain Lumley Lyster's crack pilots from the other ship feigned horror and loathing at the solid lines of the new monster. The two ships practised air strikes on one another and the odds were more or less even, for both air groups were expert units, especially in night torpedo attacks.

Homeward bound one sunny Saturday afternoon off the coast of Portugal, fire was discovered in one of *Ark*'s hangars. Luckily it was spotted before it could endanger the whole ship and dealt with energetically by Lieutenant-Commander Buckle, who made good use of the newly designed fire curtains and hangar spraying system. Even so all 812 Squadron's aircraft were destroyed.

Working up had been a happy time for the Arks, and she had proved her efficiency. Captain Power was able to tell the Institute of Naval Architects at their spring meeting that all was well with the new vessel which that great advocate of the modern carrier, Sir Arthur Johns, had inspired, and his present distinguished successor, Sir Stanley Goodall, had largely designed.

They had done their job well. For all her size the *Ark* handled superbly. 'These aircraft carriers have a very large wind area, and if the wind is on the beam and you are not moving through the water, you drift like a haystack,' complained Vice-Admiral Kennedy Purvis at the I.N.A. meeting, but Captain Power did not seem perturbed. *Ark*'s above-water form was as low and as stream-lined as it was possible for a ship of eight hundred feet to be.

Under water she gave full satisfaction too. Her design here had posed the biggest problem of all to her designers, for they faced a seeming paradox.

The above-water form was vital, to begin with. If they could not give her a long flight-deck it wasn't much use going on. But a long flight-deck implied a long hull, and a long hull did not square up at all with the demands of stability, underwater protection, and the ever-present bogey of the tonnage limitation, all of which called for beam and draught rather than length and fine lines. But they made the best compromise possible and were able to plan a shorter underwater form after all by allowing the flight-deck to overhang the stern.

They made a short ship with a long flight-deck, a fast, light ship with ample stability to ensure good manoeuvrability, and a short angle of heel when she turned so that her planes would be secure on deck. But stability must not mean bad rolling. When *Ark* crossed the Bay of Biscay in a force nine gale she did so with an easy rolling motion, the angle of roll hardly ever more than five degrees from the vertical.

She was proving herself a stiffer ship than some people had expected. Structurally speaking she was nothing but a great girder sealed at both ends. The great depth of this girder in the *Ark* meant that longitudinal stresses were not high, but athwartships she had to have more transverse frames than usual. Those two huge double-decked hangars were theoretically a weakness. Deep girders spanning their whole width had to be built in to support the upper hangar-deck and the flight deck, which had to take the shock of forces transmitted by the main structure of the ship below them, and the structure outboard of the hangar bulkheads had to be specially designed for extra strength.

The flight-deck atop of the girder was the 'strength-deck' of the whole structure, just as it was the focus of the ship's entire activity, her very raison d'être. This was where the ship's main task was begun and ended.

The ceaseless hustle and bustle of flying there throughout the spring cruise meant hard work for everybody. It kept the stewards busy, especially when the pilots were training at night, for they had to have hot food and hot drinks before they went up. And when the ship went to practise action stations the stewards themselves forgot

34

all about food and drink and went to fighting positions. Jack Burnett's action station, for example, was on an ammunition shell-hoist which supplied ammunition to the 4.5-inch guns – a long way from the wardroom pantry.

The gunners were becoming efficient, and the captain told the naval architects that his new weapons were 'very well sighted indeed.'

The bridge island itself was vitally important and had been planned with the greatest care. Some carriers of the world's navies had no island structure at all, but were entirely flush-decked like our own *Furious*, with only a tiny, telescopic navigation position to starboard and funnel pipes venting the smoke out of the ship's sides just below the level of the flight-deck. But the trend now, as embodied in the *Ark*, had set against this. Having a funnel and bridge headquarters above flight-deck level meant a cooler hangar and more room for aircraft, and a small, narrow, streamlined structure like the *Ark*'s, set well over to starboard, interfered hardly at all with the air currents over the after part of the flight-deck.

The new kind of island and roundown on *Ark* reduced eddies and air pockets, and her high speed improved the airflow down the deck, for the wind provided by the ship herself was the steadiest and most reliable for the pilots. And with the advent of low-wing monoplanes and their relative instability at low speeds the airflow was becoming more and more important. The pilots liked the island too for judging their height above the deck. 'I point the nose at the island and it's usually all right,' said one. But there was more to it than that. Pilots homed on the island psychologically as well. It was a sort of lighthouse, a homing beacon, a small skyscraper lit with welcome, a pledge of security against the treacherous nakedness of a flat, wet, pitching metal deck and limitless grey sea. Without an island to top that bare, heaving, spray-drenched deck, it could be like landing on a bleak cliff-top in an earthquake.

It was the captain's habitat, too; his home at sea and

his place of business; centre of all the life of the ship, a tower with the eyes, brain, and instincts of her being, while her great heart beat at a hundred thousand horse-power down below, moving her blindly and with a blind man's trust in the seeing eye and guiding brain above. 'It is adequate,' said Captain Power. 'I have actually spent in that island structure sixty out of the last eighty days living, sleeping, and eating, and it is adequate.'

The ship's sheer size and complexity was a joke to everyone on board. There was hardly anyone who had not been lost at one time or another. Consequently, when Ark Royal Productions, under the guiding hands of two of her pilots, Bob Everett and Ned Finch-Noyes, put on a special revue after the spring cruise, this sort of thing was highly appreciated:

'Hello, is that the switchboard? Give me long distance please, I want *Ark Royal* for'ard. . . . What's that? Take you twenty-four hours to make the necessary connection? Never mind, I'll send a fighter!'

Some of her officers did not approve of all the publicity the *Ark* was getting from the press. They did not want a '*Daily Mirror* boat' but a fighting ship. Following on the furore of her launching and commissioning as the newest thing in fighting ships, she had become a target for constant gossip and glamorising in the columns. After all she was our newest and most sensational ship of war, and war itself seemed about to involve us again. There were rumours and whispers of sabotage when news of the fire in her hangar leaked out. Then the First Lord of the Admiralty, Lord Stanhope, visited the ship, and while actually aboard made a speech in which he said that *Ark Royal*'s guns were at that very moment manned against the possibility of a surprise air attack. Of course this confidence soon spread beyond the four walls of *Ark*'s hangar and the First Lord shortly afterwards gave up his job. Captain Power did not want a bubble reputation for his ship. At this neurotic and volatile time phoney publicity was bad security for the *Ark*, the Navy, and the

Nation, and he dealt summarily with one photographer who was caught during a press visit to the ship taking forbidden shots of a Skua by immediately stopping all facilities on board until the offender had been put ashore, and only allowing the ban to be lifted when the ship was back in position. Meanwhile he summoned all the press-men and told them very bluntly exactly what he thought of such conduct in a time of grave national peril.

After Easter leave the ship went on a summer cruise to Weymouth and Torquay, taking part in the fleet regatta at Portland. In Torquay Harbour fourteen boy seamen from the ship were stranded on a sandbank, with a fleet of boats out looking for them and the weather blowing up rough. They were picked up in time and returned to the ship soaking wet.

It was midnight when they got alongside, miserably cold and soaked to the skin. Waiting at the gangway was one solitary figure. It was the captain. He was in his mess jacket and smoking his potent black tobacco. He watched them all come aboard, then gave orders that they were all to have hot soup and hot showers before they turned-in. They thought rather a lot of the captain after that.

The ship returned to Portsmouth much sooner than was expected and the ship's company were given an un-expected summer leave. The news from Europe was bad and the situation looked grave, but few of *Ark Royal*'s sailors gave it more than a passing thought, in spite of the stern fire-eating talk the captain gave them on 1st April – Hitler's birthday.

Significantly, more key men had been drafted to the ship over the summer months. Some had joined her after her return from the Mediterranean.

John Coward joined from R.N.B. He had been joining ships in a steady stream ever since that day in 1925 when he had thrown over a good job ashore to work for the firm that owned all the ships.

'Where have you been?' asked the manager that day.

'Joining the Royal Navy, sir!' said John, and was sacked on the spot.

Since then he had served in the battleships *Malaya*, *Warspite*, *Valiant*, and *Queen Elizabeth*; the cruisers *Cornwall* and *London*, and small ships like the little sloop *Wild Swan*. Then, in April 1939, his 'manager' sent for him again. This time it was the drafting commander, and it wasn't to give him the sack.

'I'm sending you to the *Ark Royal* for twelve months,' he said, 'owing to the shortage of qualified petty officer cooks. I shall call you in after twelve months as I notice you have done a good deal of sea time.' Of course he could hardly have been expected to allow for Hitler.

Coward's first reaction to the *Ark* was, 'Where do we go from here?' He thought it was rather like trying to find his way about London – he was a West Countryman.

Percy Hancock, petty officer telegraphist, had joined the Navy about the same time as Coward, and he too had put in plenty of sea time, having picked up his petty officer's rate in the *Hood*. After the *Hood* he went to the Signals School at Portsmouth as an instructor. One day in July 1939 he took his class aboard the *Ark Royal*, which had just put in from Torquay and Portland, to have a look at her radio installations. A month later he himself was drafted aboard her to relieve the senior petty officer telegraphist, who was due to go to pension.

The Chief never went to pension. He went instead, after summer leave, with the ship to Scottish waters.

Ark's first call was Invergordon. From here they went north to Scapa Flow. There, in that vast, historic anchorage, where the mighty dreadnoughts of the Grand Fleet had once ridden at anchor, they found other ships of the Home Fleet. Here were the ships of the 2nd Battle Squadron, *Nelson*, *Rodney*, *Royal Oak*, *Royal Sovereign* and *Ramillies*, and the battlecruisers *Hood* and *Repulse*; the 18th Cruiser Squadron, *Aurora*, *Sheffield*, *Edinburgh*, and *Belfast*; the 12th Cruiser Squadron, *Effingham*, *Emerald*, *Cardiff*, and *Dunedin*; the 7th Cruiser Squadron,

Diomede, Dragon, Calypso, and *Caledon*; the seventeen destroyers of the 6th and 8th Flotillas; the minesweepers of the 1st Minesweeping Flotilla. By 31st August *Ark Royal* had come to complete the array. Other ships of the Home Fleet were disposed around our coasts; the *Furious* was at Rosyth; there was a flotilla of submarines at Dundee, and another at Blyth; in the Humber were the *Southampton* and *Glasgow* of the 2nd Cruiser Squadron; at Portland the battleships *Resolution* and *Revenge*, the carriers *Courageous* and *Hermes*, the cruisers *Ceres, Caradoc*, and *Cairo*, and the 18th Destroyer Flotilla. Other groups of destroyers and small craft were stationed at various important ports around Britain.

The Home Fleet was under the command of Admiral Sir Charles Forbes. Although far less powerful than the Grand Fleet of 1914, the Home Fleet of 1939 was the strongest of all our fleets, for if war broke out the defence of our home waters would be the Royal Navy's most important commitment. In the naval war plans approved by the Board of Admiralty on 30th January the Commander-in-Chief, Home Fleet, was ordered 'to close the North Sea to all movements of enemy shipping and to exercise contraband control of neutral shipping'.

On the evening of 31st August, with all his ships assembled and ready in their war positions, Admiral Forbes put to sea to patrol the area between the Shetlands and Norway. Aircraft from the *Ark Royal* helped in the search for U-boats or any other sign of warlike activity.

Next day the Admiralty reported that some German ships had broken out of the North Sea and were in Icelandic waters. In fact they were ten days late with their information. On 21st August the pocket battleship *Graf Spee* had sailed to a war position in the Atlantic, to be followed by the *Deutschland* three days later. At the same time two supply ships, the *Altmark* and *Wester-wald*, put to sea to support them. During this period we had no air reconnaissance up over the area and the

German ships got through in complete secrecy. A number of U-boats also sailed for positions around the British Isles.

On the same day, 1st September, one of *Ark Royal*'s Swordfish, watching the waters off the Norwegian coast, ran into a fog bank and became lost. The pilot dived to clear the fog. When they broke clear they found themselves flying over a fiord. There was nowhere to land ashore, and they could not turn back through the fog, so the pilot force-landed on the water.

When the Swordfish hit the water they lost no time in breaking out the rubber dinghy and began paddling ashore, watching their aircraft slowly sink and disappear in the icy waters. Shivering and gloomy they scrambled ashore, certain that war was only a matter of hours away – if it had not been declared already – and that they were doomed to go 'into the bag' for the duration in a neutral country.

They told their sad story to the Norwegian Air Force officers who gave them a much-needed meal and change of clothes. As fellow airmen they were intensely sympathetic.

'Don't worry,' the miserable young men were told, 'there is no war yet. We will fly you to Bergen and you can get the boat to England from there.'

So they climbed into a seaplane, were flown to Bergen, and were on the high seas between Norway and the Tyne on that fateful Sunday morning of 3rd September, wishing they were back on the *Ark.* . . .

The *Ark* had a patrol of Swordfish up as usual that morning. Up in his cold open cockpit Bob Everett shivered and wondered when somebody would get round to issuing Swordfish aircrews with proper fur-lined flying jackets. The Skua crews had them, of course, in their warm closed cockpits. . . . Just like the Navy!

He was glad to land-on again at the end of the patrol, and climbed stiffly out of the cockpit longing for a slice of gin and the warmth of the wardroom bar.

An officer passed by. 'Hello,' he said casually. 'War's been declared. Did you know?'

'Has it?' said Everett, with equal apparent disinterest, far too cold and browned off for the news to sink in.

The information had reached the ship just after eleven o'clock. Dick Christopher, on watch all day in the Signal Distributing Office, where they had to cope with a stream of wireless messages flooding in almost incessantly from the Admiralty, was to remember that one, all-important message.

It came addressed to Vice-Admiral, Aircraft Carriers, Vice-Admiral Wells, who wore his flag in the *Ark*.

The envelope came up the pneumatic tube from the wireless office. The Flag Lieutenant took it at once to the Admiral.

Then the Swordfish of the morning patrol started coming aboard and everybody was far too busy to think about anything else.

A few minutes after the last Swordfish of the flight had been struck-down into the hangar the wail of the bosun's pipe was heard over the Tannoy throughout the ship.

'D'ye hear there! D'ye hear there!' came the rasping voice of the bosun's mate. There was a pause. Then they heard the captain say.

'This is the captain speaking. I have just received the signal "Commence hostilities at once with Germany." '

The Home Fleet immediately instituted the blockade of Germany. Coastal Command aircraft began their search of the sea for enemy shipping, greatly handicapped by lack of numbers, and submarines took up their stations along those stretches of the patrol lines which were beyond the range of the inadequate Ansons which Coastal Command had to use at this stage. The cruisers *Southampton* and *Glasgow* and eight destroyers from the Humber cruised off the Norwegian coast.

Admiral Forbes, with the main body of the Home Fleet, patrolled the North Atlantic. They were looking for enemy ships, and one ship in particular. The famous

41

liner *Bremen* was known to be on passage home from New York. But the *Bremen* had not won the Blue Riband for nothing. When the Home Fleet were looking for her four hundred miles west of the Hebrides she was already in Murmansk.

On the evening of their fruitless search the Home Fleet received a signal from the Admiralty reporting that the German Fleet had put to sea. At full speed the fleet retraced its steps and steamed east into the North Sea through the Fair Isle Channel.

They cruised, ready for battle, in thick fog, off the Orkneys until the morning of 6th September, when they returned to Scapa Flow.

Next day, Admiral Forbes sailed again with *Nelson, Rodney, Repulse, Ark Royal, Aurora, Sheffield,* and ten destroyers to patrol the Norwegian coast in search of enemy shipping. On 8th September the *Hood, Renown,* two cruisers and four destroyers left to patrol between Iceland and the Faroes. The weather was appalling and neither force saw anything. On 10th September the main body returned to Scapa, followed two days later by the *Hood* squadron.

So far no U-boats had been sighted by our warships and none of the ships of the Home Fleet had been attacked by them. That Nazi Germany did not intend to use them at least as savagely as the Kaiser had done was a dim hope. Soon they must show themselves. Soon, too, the powerful heavy ships of the German Navy must surely put to sea to attack our merchant shipping – those which were not already out.

CHAPTER III

'WHERE IS THE *ARK ROYAL*?'

'IN order to bridge the gap of two or three weeks between the outbreak of war and the completion of new auxiliary anti-U-boat flotillas, we had decided to use the aircraft carriers with some freedom in helping to bring in the unarmed, unorganised, and unconvoyed traffic which was then approaching our shores in large numbers. This was a risk which it was right to run.'

It was a bold calculated risk of Mr Churchill's to use our few priceless carriers, each with a few destroyers, in this way, especially *Ark Royal*, our newest and finest.

One of the earliest results was that a certain U-boat captain at approximately twenty minutes to three on the afternoon of 14th September looked into his periscope, tense with suppressed excitement, hardly able to believe his luck.

'*Ark Royal!*' he said.

The great ship was heeling, helpless and vulnerable, having just flown off three Skuas. . . .

That day Signalman Dick Christopher was second

hand of the watch with Leading-Signalman Nobby Hall as the leading hand. Dick had just made a jug of tea in the little signal house on the flag deck.

'Hey, Nobby!' he shouted. 'Come and have a cup!'

But Nobby did not answer. Dick looked out and saw him leaning over the rail, staring out over the water.

Suddenly he whipped round and shouted,

'Torpedoes in sight!'

Then he leaped to the admiral's and officer of the watch's voice pipes and shouted again his urgent report. The ship altered course, heeling sharply. Dick saw plainly the warheads of two torpedoes breaking surface as they raced towards the ship.

Thanks to Nobby the *Ark* combed their tracks. They exploded a hundred yards off the stern and scattered smoking metal over the after end of the flight-deck.

Most men would have sunk back then and left it to somebody else. But Nobby Hall had not finished. On his own initiative he manned the 24-inch searchlight signalling projector and flashed the code signal which meant 'Hunt for enemy submarine' to the destroyers, which were only dots on the horizon. The destroyers closed at full speed.

The U-boat went deep, sliding down into the green fathoms to hide. But she was not quick enough. There was a great clap of explosive thunder as the first pattern of depth-charges went up almost alongside her hull. The lights went out in the submarine's whole long, cluttered spaces and all the atoms in her structure seemed to leap apart.

It was like being in a darkened tube train deep in the earth with the ground quaking and detonating all around. From the engine room aft came shouts and screams. The main engines had been jerked clean off their beds. Deadly chlorine gas from the batteries began to fill the boat.

Rending this dark world of horror under the sea came the shock of the second pattern. The submarine shook wildly and tilted. Foaming white water burst through a hundred cracks and torn pipes. But she was surfacing.

As she came up the layers on the destroyer *Faulkner* read the white letters 'U-39' on her conning tower and pressed their triggers. Then one man, then another and another stumbled frantically out of the U-boat's conning-tower hatch, and soon her whole ship's company were throwing themselves into the grey, choppy water. As the last man took to the water the conning-tower slowly disappeared behind him, there was an uprush of air and a white, silent explosion of bubbles, and a bit of Hitler's frightfulness was no more.

The *Faulkner* picked up the survivors and Nobby Hall read with satisfaction the signal she made to *Ark Royal* reporting U-39 sunk and the forty-three members of her ship's company made prisoner. The captured Germans had to be persuaded that they would not be shot or tortured for information.

Meanwhile the three Skuas which had taken off just before the fight were fighting an action of their own.

They had found what they were looking for. That morning the *Ark* had received an SOS from the steamer *Fanad Head* saying that she had been torpedoed in a position two hundred miles away to the south-west.

The Skuas found her as she lay stopped in the water, her lifeboats scattered round on the sea. The airmen could see the yellow flowers of shell bursts blossoming on her hull, and the dark shape of the U-boat which was trying to finish her off with gunfire.

The pilots pushed their sticks forward, kicked their rudders hard, and went down. The German crash-dived. Her gun-crews trod water and had a fish's-eye view of the fight.

One after the other Skuas released their bombs and climbed away. Two of them went so low that the exploding bombs shattered the after part of each aircraft, killing the air-gunners and dashing the pilots into the sea. They took to their rubber dinghies and watched the surviving

Skua climb away. The next thing they saw was the humped shape of the U-30 surface slowly on the *Fanad Head*'s starboard quarter. The Skua saw her and dived again, machine-gunning the submarine's conning-tower and forcing her below once more. Then she circled the wretched airmen in their little heaving rubber boats and returned to the *Ark*.

She sent six Swordfish to the scene a little later, who found the U-boat firing a torpedo at the stubborn merchantman. All six went down and bombed her, not knowing that their two shipmates were now prisoners on board the U-boat. They saw several bombs hit and returned to the *Ark* to report a sinking.

In fact the U-boat survived, as we discovered later when she put one of her wounded seamen ashore in Iceland. The bombs which had hit her had been too ineffectual to disable her. The luckless Skua pilots became the first men of the Fleet Air Arm to go into captivity as prisoners of war, and the two air-gunners her first casualties. *Ark Royal*'s destroyers finally swept the board clean by picking up the *Fanad Head*'s passengers and crew from her lifeboats.

It looked as though Mr Churchill's calculated risk was beginning to pay off. As he wrote later of the attack on the *Ark Royal*, 'mercifully the torpedoes missed, and her assailant was promptly sunk. . . . '

But it had been a very near thing. While the *Ark* and her group were U-boat hunting the First Lord had been inspecting the Home Fleet in Scapa Flow and in the new anchorage of Lock Ewe in Western Scotland, which the Home Fleet had begun to use on 9th September as a temporary refuge from German bombers raiding Scapa.

On the morning of his return to London he was surprised to see the First Sea Lord, Sir Dudley Pound, on the platform at Euston. Pound said,

'I have bad news for you, First Lord. The *Courageous* was sunk yesterday in the Bristol Channel.'

It was particularly sad news for the *Ark Royal*'s squadron's, who had lived and worked in the old ship. She had suffered the fate which the *Ark* herself had so narrowly missed. A U-boat had come upon her as she was turning into wind to receive aircraft and sent her to the bottom with heavy loss of life.

Now there were only four of our big carriers left. Each one was a top priority target for U-boat and bomber, especially when she was pre-occupied with flying off or taking aboard aircraft.

Whenever Forbes put to sea with the main body of the Home Fleet the *Ark Royal* went with him, her planes scouting ahead of the battleships and searching the sea for signs of U-boats. We had little enough air power to cover the northern seas, and the carrier's aircraft were priceless, although the Admiralty was cautious in probing their potentialities at this time. The idea still seemed prevalent in some quarters that the big gun was king and aeroplanes were mobile kite-balloons useful for scouting purposes. Their use as 'extended artillery' had yet to be realised. It was infuriating for her pilots to have to stand on deck staring helplessly at the sky, waiting for enemy bombers to attack, while their own machines lay down in the hangars drained of fuel for fear of fire, and *Ark Royal* staggered along in the wake of the cumbersome *Nelson* and *Rodney*, which could only make eighteen knots. To use a potential battle winner as a floating anti-aircraft battery for the protection of the battleships seemed to them the height of big-gun stupidity.

This sort of old-fashioned thinking planned still in terms of the comparatively short-range slogging match between rival fleets of dreadnoughts. Many failed to realise, and some actively resented, the power of the aeroplane in locating and attacking ships in hitherto inaccessible places over long distances, just as bomber partisans often exaggerated the power of the aircraft to destroy warships well defended by carrier-borne fighters and anti-aircraft guns.

It seemed as if some of our admirals dreamed of another Jutland and a chance this time of smashing the power of the German Navy beyond all dispute. This our dreadnoughts had failed to do at Jutland. But we still had a few of these monolithic monsters left, plus one or two rather more modern versions of 'Fisher's folly'. Now, thought the ironclad veterans, is the time to use them, while the German capital ships are few in number, and before they can get the mighty *Bismarck* and *Tirpitz* ready.

On 22nd September the Home Fleet put to sea. Ahead of them, with the intention of making a raid into the Skagerrak, went the 2nd Cruiser Squadron, comprising *Southampton*, *Glasgow*, *Sheffield*, and *Aurora*, and eight destroyers. Fleet veterans remembered the similar move which had drawn the German High Seas Fleet out of its harbours in 1916 and culminated in the Jutland battle.

But whether Jutland would have been fought again and what the outcome would have been will never be known. On 23rd September a collision between two destroyers of the Humber force compelled the whole fleet to return to Scapa.

On 25th September a signal came in reporting the submarine *Spearfish* badly damaged in the Skagerrak and unable to dive. The C.-in-C. immediately sent the 2nd Cruiser Squadron to her rescue, while the battle cruisers and the 18th Cruiser Squadron were ordered to act as a covering force, and the battleships as deeper support.

It was a disposition of forces similar to the arrangement which brought on Jutland. Perhaps the Germans would fall into the trap again.

The Nazis, however, had learned the lesson of air power. Instead of risking their precious new battle cruisers against our fleet they sent the Luftwaffe, and almost caught the Home Fleet with its hands tied behind its back. But for the bad weather and the luck and skill

of the *Ark* they might have rubbed the lesson in severely
and really made it hurt.

They sent out a flight of Dornier 18 flying-boats to
shadow the carrier and the battleships early on the morning of 26th September. The Dorniers picked them up and
tried to hold on to them in the misty, cloudy weather.
The British ships knew they were being watched and were
uneasy, their men searching grey sky and sea for signs of
trouble. But cloud hid the Dorniers. A flight of Skuas was
ordered up from *Ark Royal* to find them.

When Lieutenant Charles Evans, a dashing, fiery sailor,
and one of the Navy's finest fighter pilots, led them off
the deck they knew the enemy were close. They left the
Ark with a flourish and a whirl of last-minute preparation.
Evans found himself without his regular observer, so
Petty Officer Cunningham, a rating observer from the
same squadron, was told, 'Hop in and go with them!'

McEwan and Petty Officer Brian Seymour, the senior
telegraphist-air-gunner of the squadron, did not normally
fly together either, but today they made up a pair.

Seymour was busy right up to the last moment organising first the other telegraphist-air-gunners and then himself. A T.A.G.'s work was never done at the best of
times, let alone in this mad rush. He had to be responsible for getting all the information of the position of
ships in the vicinity, the call-signs and codes of the day,
and for looking after the observers' gear. He not only
had to work the aircraft's radio and transmit and receive
signals in the air, but he also had to maintain the set in
first-class working order. If the set failed in the air, the
T.A.G. was on the bridge in front of the captain when he
got down. And he had to be an air-gunner as well. Just
to add insult to injury, because he was only a rating he
had no special rest-room like the commissioned pilots
and observers, and no special hot meal laid on before a
patrol, as they did. He just had to do it all and lump it.
The Admiralty seemed to know about as much of the

modern technique of air warfare and of the special needs of aircrews as Nelson did, with slightly less excuse.

Th Skuas took off and circled *Nelson, Rodney,* and *Ark,* the pilots, gunners, and observers straining their eyes through the gloom and murk for signs of the enemy.

Suddenly they saw a dark, mottled shape low on the water.

They dived towards it. It was a flying-boat, cleverly camouflaged in blue, green, and grey. A Dornier.

The Skuas attacked, one after the other. First the pilot would open up with his four Brownings, then the T.A.G. or observer raked the German with his Lewis, with the Dornier firing back all the time.

After each Skua had made two attacks they saw the Dornier go down and flop into the water like a wounded duck. McEwan went down to look closely at him. He heard Seymour's guns start firing.

'Leave him alone,' he said, 'he's down now.'

'Yes, but his engines are still turning,' said the T.A.G. He thought the German might be foxing. If his engines were all right he might be able to take off again.

Then the Dornier's propellers stopped. They saw tiny figures climbing out of the cockpits. One of them waved something white in the air. 'Looks like a pair of white overalls,' thought Brian Seymour irrelevantly.

The Germans broke out their rubber dinghy and one man got into it. The little float heaved up and down in the choppy water, and before the other could climb into it it was washed away from the flying-boat's side. Two men were left stranded on the Dornier. Then the machine sank and they had to swim for it.

McEwan and Seymour reported back to *Ark Royal* and said at de-briefing that they thought their bullets had hit. Otherwise they thought little more about the incident. They were rather more interested in the bullet holes they found in the engine of their Skua.

McEwan's old L2873 was an historic aircraft and in it

50

they themselves had made history, although they did not know it until someone told them after the war.

Of course there was great jubilation after the victory. The squadron aircrews, all of whom had eventually gone up that morning, had a Black Velvet party, at which the champagne ran out long before the stout. It was *Ark Royal*'s first aircraft victory and they all drank to it as the result of a combined effort.

More than that, however, 803 Squadron's Dornier was the first enemy aircraft of the whole war to be shot down by any of our forces.

'The *Ark* did that – and anybody else can put it in their pipe and smoke it!' was *Ark Royal*'s own reaction.

Meanwhile everybody on deck was feeling cold and hungry. The weather was beginning to blow up and the visibility deteriorating even further. Those off watch had fortified themselves against the cold with their daily tot or a big gin. A few lucky ones on watch had oppos who had struggled up to their action stations from the mess with those precious gulpers that enfused warmth through a chilled body.

It was pretty obvious that the Dorniers that had got away would bring trouble sooner or later. Lookouts watched their sectors of sky intently, gunners absent-mindedly fingered B.M. levers and firing triggers, pilots and air-gunners on patrol shivered and cursed.

The ships in the force well knew they were in for trouble. Sixteen hundred men in *Ark Royal* who had been at action stations all that day in the dreary grey cold waited for the Germans to come to them.

The padre visited all the exposed positions at the guns, on the flight-deck and on the bridge, with piles of corned beef sandwiches and fannies of hot cocoa. That put every one in a better mood.

Still no attack materialised, and about two o'clock some of the men were allowed a stand-easy. Dick Christopher and one or two other signalmen were told they could go below for half an hour. They went down and stretched out on the tables and mess stools for a short nap.

Jack Bishop's gun's crew were fallen out to get dinner. Jack himself went to the galley to get the dinner for his mess.

In the wardroom McEwan, who had just got down from that successful morning's work, sat down to lunch. He stared somewhat distastefully at a large helping of baked beans.

At his gun station on XI Ron Hornsby was manning the communications phone. He blew on his hands and cursed the cold and the everlasting grey, miserable sea.

Up on the range-finder Able-Seaman Parham, called 'Nippy' because he had driven a steam-roller in civilian life, turned round quietly to the range officer and pointed.

'Look, sir,' he said, 'a Jerry.'

'That's a Hudson,' said the officer. They had all been watching with keen interest one of the new Hudson aircraft of Coastal Command, the first they had ever seen.

'What, with bloody great kisses on!' said Nippy.

The machine – somebody said 'It's a Heinkel' – lunged roaring out of the low cloud. Its guns hammered out and Ron Hornsby ducked as bullets whanged and whined about the gun position aft. All the guns themselves opened up at once.

The men on the bridge watched him release his bombs. The huge two-thousand pounder came tumbling down.

'Like my Austin Seven,' thought one officer incongruously.

'More like a London bus,' he decided swiftly as it got bigger.

With his eye on the bomb Captain Power gave the swift wheel order which turned the *Ark* sharply to starboard.

Then the bomb burst.

A huge wall of white water rose and crashed and spilled over the for'ard end of the flight-deck as *Ark* lifted bodily upwards and lurched viciously to starboard.

Below, the whole world reeled and crashed and everything loose tore away and skittered wildly across the deck.

In the wardroom McEwan gaped numbly at a lapful of baked beans.

Jack Bishop, the dish containing hot food in his hands, was caught halfway down the messdeck ladder. He was thrown the rest of the way and ended up on his behind on the deck with the mess's dinner all over him. He leapt up and clanged up the ladder back to the gun, trailing gravy and pusser's peas.

The terrible bang threw Dick Christopher off the mess table. The whole ship's side bulged in and out again and they were all flung in a heap on the deck, with gash buckets upending over them and spilling the garbage everywhere. Their mess was on the water line so they did not loiter, but made the upper deck in record time.

The ship rolled and shuddered, the bows seemed to reel in the air, then she settled again in a series of shuddering spasms with a list to starboard which finally righted itself until she was on an even keel once more.

Those rushing up from below got on deck just in time to see the tail of the Heinkel disappearing in the distance. It was a *very* near miss and the captain's wheel order had saved the ship. It shook her ship's company into the full realisation 'there's a war on!'

The whole force opened up and guns were going off wildly everywhere.

'For goodness' sake pull yourself together!' signalled Admiral Tovey to his ships. It was their first taste of war in the air.

Anything the remotest bit fragile aboard *Ark Royal* was shattered by the bomb. Cups and empty cocoa fannies flew over the side or shot into the air to land on the heads of the men on deck. Signal pads, signalling flags, binoculars, all did the same wild dance in the air and caused one or two headaches when they landed. The searchlight reflector was shattered and joiner Sid Tanner had to build an enormous packing case to send it away in.

Those at their action stations below decks were the worst off of all. Chef John Coward was at action stations on the ammunition hoist just below the flight-deck and was too busy to ask what was going on. Cyril Calder down in the transmitting station heard the noise and felt the terrible shock and was certain they had been mortally hit. The *Hood* was narrowly missed as well. Watchers in the *Ark* saw a bomb explode so close alongside her that a broad patch of grey paint was peeled off her side, revealing the red lead underneath.

On the way back to Scapa Flow the ships remained on the alert and there was intensive gun drill.

Things seemed quiet just before they got into Scapa and the *Ark*'s gunners were practising with dummy ammunition. An air-raid developed unfortunately just as they began and *Ark Royal* was caught with dummy ammunition in the breech. The gunner's mate, popularly known as Lignum Vitae, had his leg pulled mercilessly at tot time.

When they did get in they were glad of a stand-easy. The ship's broadcasting system was turned on, for the Arks were very fond of music and ran their own 'disc jockey' programme. They were enjoying the music when the programme was suddenly switched on to another wavelength.

'*Gar*many calling. . . . *Gar*many calling. . . . '

It was Lord Haw-Haw, the Irishman William Joyce.

'Turn that crap off!' said someone.

Then they heard something which made them listen with all attention. *What* was that he said?

'Where is the *Ark Royal*?' asked that sneering voice.

A boot flew through the air and hit the loudspeaker.

'We're here, you bastard!' they all sang out together.

It was the first time they had heard the question which was to be repeated ad nauseam throughout the following months by Goebbels' propaganda ministry. From this time on little Goebbels sank the *Ark Royal* every day, like a venomous, club-footed Walter Mitty.

For a while the Luftwaffe thought they really had sunk her. Lance-Corporal Francke, pilot of the Heinkel that had very nearly done so, was not certain and only reported that he had bombed a British carrier in the North Sea and scored either a hit or a very near miss. But nobody listened to him. His report was torn up and Germany and the whole world were told what Goebbels wanted them to believe.

'Heart of Our Attack – The Aircraft Carrier!'

So ran the headline in the Nazi Party paper *Volkischer Beobachter*. Underneath was an 'artist's impression' of the great carrier cavorting out of the water, shattered and writhing, with mountainous columns of flame and smoke everywhere. In the bottom right-hand corner an odd-looking battleship was depicted suffering a similar fate. Other papers printed the headlines of the *Ark Royal*'s sinking in red. Lurid pictures of 'the end of the *Ark Royal*' were carried by all the magazines, and the wretched Francke was forced to put his name to a thousand fictitious accounts of that afternoon in the North Sea. The Ministry of Propaganda even brought out a boy's book called *How I Sank the* Ark Royal – with pictures.

Goering sent Francke a personal telegram of congratulations, decorated him with the Iron Cross, and promoted him to Oberleutnant. But the officers' mess received him with derision and his life was made a misery. He confided in an American journalist that he was thinking of committing suicide. The American suggested that a very quick way of doing this would be to make the truth available to the free press of the world. But Francke preferred to live on and survived his attack of conscience, only to be killed later on on the Eastern Front.

Another American helped to nail the Nazi lie. Immediately after the 'news' of the *Ark*'s sinking began to issue from the German radio, which broadcast its damaging lies all over the world, Captain Allan G. Kirk, the United States Naval Attaché at the American Embassy in London, paid an official visit to Admiral Sir Charles Forbes, Commander-in-Chief of the Home Fleet. Said *The Times* on 3rd October, 'Captain Kirk was present on Sunday during the regular church services in the *Ark Royal*, and he observed all the normal Sunday routine of the fleet, including the mustering of the crews of the ships and the conduct of church services throughout the fleet. The normal force of the entire fleet, including every one of the capital ships, was present. All the ships of the fleet were seen by Captain Kirk to be in perfect condition, undamaged in any part by the German air attack. No ship had been hit by the bombs during that attack and no casualties had been received.'

That Sunday night a certain Herr Fritsche on the German radio demanded that the world should be told, as he said, 'the truth about the *Ark Royal*'. Captain Kirk heard the request from one of *Ark Royal*'s loudspeakers, sitting in her wardroom surrounded by a crowd of her grinning officers. As soon as he returned to London he obliged Herr Fritsche by making a routine report to the Navy Department in Washington describing his visit to the 'sunken' carrier.

And on the same Sunday night the free world heard Mr Churchill say,

'The Royal Navy is hunting the U-boats night and day and we hope by the end of October to have three times as many hunting craft at work as at the beginning of the war. The Government is inevitably resolved to make the maximum effort of which the British nation is capable, and to persevere whatever may happen, until decisive victory is gained.'

Captain Kirk's report and repeated Admiralty denials notwithstanding, the Germans went on demanding that the First Lord of the Admiralty should tell the world 'the truth about the *Ark Royal*'. Herr Fritsche informed Mr

Churchill, 'The Germany of National Socialism now raps you over the knuckles to the amusement of the whole world.'

But soon the laugh was on Herr Fritsche, for the *Ark Royal* would not stay sunk.

CHAPTER IV

FLYING DUTCHMAN

ON 2nd October the fleet was in Loch Ewe. During the first dog-watch a flag signal was hoisted by the Commander-in-Chief in *Nelson*. It was addressed to *Renown* and *Ark Royal*, and ordered them to raise steam for full speed by 1800 hours. When they were well out to sea Captain Power spoke to *Ark*'s ship's company over the loudspeaker system and told them that the next land they would see would be Sierra Leone.

On the previous day a number of survivors from the steamer *Clement* had reached the coast of South America. They reported that their ship had been sunk by the pocket battleship *Admiral Scheer* on 30th September.

The news confirmed Admiralty suspicions that there was a German raider loose in the South Atlantic. Immediately they set about forming a number of powerful hunting groups to track her down. Heavy cruisers *Berwick* and *York*, as Force F, were ordered down from Halifax, Nova Scotia, to patrol North American and West Indian waters. *Exeter* and *Cumberland*, as Force

G, already in the South Atlantic, began a patrol of the south-east coast of America, and were joined later by the light cruisers *Ajax* and *Achilles*. Two more heavy cruisers, *Sussex* and *Shropshire*, as Force H, were sent from the Mediterranean to the Cape of Good Hope area, and *Cornwall* and *Dorsetshire*, with the carrier *Eagle*, as Force I, were moved to Ceylon from the China station. *Ark Royal* and *Renown*, designated Force K, came from the Home Fleet to search the Pernambuco area. At Brest Force L, the battleship *Dunkerque*, the carrier *Béarn*, and three French six-inch cruisers, were alerted for the chase, and two more eight-inch French cruisers, as Force M, searched from their base at Dakar. Finally, the carrier *Hermes* came from Plymouth to join the French battlecruiser *Strasbourg* in patrolling the West Indies, as Force N.

There were thus eight groups of powerful ships, including four carriers, in the process of formation. The heart of the whole complex was formed by the groups G (*Exeter*, *Cumberland*, and later *Ajax* and *Achilles*), H (*Sussex* and *Shropshire*), and K (*Ark Royal* and *Renown*). It was upon these ships that the heaviest burden of searching fell, the weary days of patrol in the South Atlantic wastes. They were placed under the operational control of the Commander-in-Chief, South Atlantic, Admiral G. H. d'Oyly Lyon, with his headquarters at Freetown. He was also allowed to retain four destroyers which had previously been ordered home. In addition to the formation of the main hunter groups, the battleships *Resolution* and *Revenge*, the cruisers *Enterprise* and *Emerald*, and later the *Warspite*, *Repulse*, and *Furious*, were sent to Halifax to escort homeward-bound Atlantic convoys, the *Malaya* and *Glorious* were despatched from the Mediterranean to the Indian Ocean.

All these dispositions were made to trap, as it was then thought, the *Admiral Scheer*. There were many ships in the hunt, but none too many to catch a clever raider who was now at large in the vast blue-and-grey wasteland of the southern oceans, pursuing a trade at which the German Navy were past masters. The Admiralty had estimated that we would need a bare minimum of seventy cruisers to deal with our commitments at sea in wartime. Of these we had only fifty-eight. We could have done with those missing twelve ships now in the South Atlantic. And, of course, we could have used more carriers and search planes. A task force of modern carriers, similar to those formed later by the U.S. Navy in the Pacific and eventually by our own Pacific Fleet, might have brought the raider swiftly to book. As it was, the only modern carrier available was the *Ark Royal*. Her aircraft would have to be flown to the utmost limits of their endurance.

On 5th October, when *Ark Royal* was only three days out from Loch Ewe on passage to Freetown, the raider was heard from again. The s.s. *Newton Beach* sent out distress signals which were picked up by another ship and passed to the cruiser *Cumberland*. *Cumberland* unfortunately presumed that the message had also been passed to Admiral Lyon at Freetown, and did not consider it worth breaking wireless silence to relay it to him. In fact Lyon had not received the message. If *Cumberland* had informed him, the raider and her supply ship might well have been caught within a few days. We learned later that she had already had one life on 11th September, when her seaplane had warned her in time of the close proximity of the *Cumberland*, which she sighted thirty miles away on passage from Freetown to Rio. On the same day that the *Newton Beach* was sunk, the s.s. *Stonegate* also fell in with a German raider and was sent to the bottom.

Four days after the sinking of the *Newton Beach* and *Stonegate*, patrolling planes from *Ark Royal* sighted a ship stopped west of the Cape Verde Islands. When challenged the mysterious vessel claimed to be the s.s. *Delmar*, an American ship. Vice-Admiral Wells, in

Ark Royal, decided not to investigate further, as he had no destroyers with him and was wary of U-boats. Too late it was discovered that the s.s. *Delmar* was in New Orleans. The imposter was the German supply ship *Altmark.*

Between the 5th October, when the *Newton Beach* was sunk, and the 10th, three more ships were sunk on the trade routes from the Cape. Then several days passed without further incident, vital days which gave the Germans ample time to rendezvous with the supply ship which *Ark Royal* had let slip through her hands, and be off again to any of a hundred fruitful corners of the Atlantic or Indian Oceans.

On 12th October Force K arrived at Freetown in blistering heat. There had been no time to lay in any tropical gear before sailing from Scotland, and officers and men were hard put to find anything cool enough. One of *Ark*'s signalmen, Leading-Signalman Christian, was very badly sunburned on his arms through having to read and pass semaphore signals for two hours while *Ark Royal* and *Renown* were proceeding to the anchorage. Shore leave in Freetown was not encouraged, and indeed there was nothing worth going ashore for. The steamy heat rose early from the swamps and fired the air to a sweltering, humid intensity. As usual, *Ark Royal*'s ship's company managed to get their fun on board ship. All the local dignitaries visited them, exotically dressed in peacock apparel, and a regimental band of the King's African Rifles 'beat retreat' on the flight-deck.

Force K was not here to show the flag, however, but put out very soon to look for the raider. Then began a period of intense, monotonous ocean searches by the Swordfish from the *Ark.*

'An aircraft flying over the South Atlantic,' said one of her pilots afterwards, 'is the most solitary object in the world. It ranges the sky as lonely as a cloud, beyond the view of its fellows or its parent ship. Hour after hour would go by without the sight of so much as a soap-box, yet each member of the crew had to keep constantly alert.'

Lieutenant Bob Everett used to shout down the Gosport tube to his observer, Australian 'Digger' Gerrett, 'Don't forget to talk to me now and again. It's the only way I shall be able to stay awake!'

Twice a day, day after day, a patrol took off, one at dawn and another after lunch, on a patient, painstaking plod over the biggest slab of sea in the world, flying endlessly on towards a limitless horizon which never yielded that tell-tale wisp of smoke. Besides these constant searches two Swordfish kept up a constant patrol over Force K itself, being relieved every two or three hours. About all they received for their pains was chronic pins and needles in the bottom.

The Skuas suffered from the opposite complaint. They could never get *enough* time in the air, for there was nothing for them to bomb and nothing to fight. Sometimes they were allowed to vent their frustration by making mock attacks on the Swordfish returning from patrol or by dummy strikes on the ships to give the gun-crews some practice, and occasionally they were used for some of the less ambitious recces.

On these happy occasions they would come up on the lifts from their dark recesses in the lower hangar and their pilots and gunners would emerge, pale and blinking, on to the flight-deck and their hibernation below like pit ponies into the blessed light of day. In fact that is what the Swordfish pilots called them. The 'pit ponies' of the *Ark* were to have their day, however, although that day was not at hand yet. They were never allowed out of sight of the ship. 'All right,' the captain would say, 'you can go up and form fours or whatever it is you do!' Then off went the Skuas. But if one of them so much as disappeared for a moment in a cloud the captain would have them recalled immediately.

Life on board was made as pleasant as possible with deck hockey, quiz games, cinema shows, and concerts given by Ark Royal Productions. It had always been a boast of *Ark Royal* that her men did not need to go ashore for entertainment. In fact they never seemed to get the chance, with week after week at sea and only Freetown, the white man's grave, with its one pub, the City Bar, at the end of it all.

There was one blessing. Out here they were free of Lord Haw-Haw, who went on blackening the *Ark*'s good name and obstinately implying that her Swordfish were searching for the *Scheer* on the bottom of the North Sea. On 10th October a Rotterdam paper reported that Lance-Corporal Francke had been promoted and awarded the Iron Cross, both 1st and 2nd class, 'for sinking the *Ark Royal*'. On 15th October a Danish paper said, 'According to German estimates the English Fleet has now suffered a certain loss of 70,000 tons – namely, two aircraft carriers, the *Royal Oak* and a 10,000 ton cruiser. . . . German aircraft are equipped with a wonderful bomb-aiming instrument far superior to anything else known. It is manufactured by Zeiss of Jena.' The *Royal Oak*, alas, *had* been lost, but the other lie had simply grown bigger and bigger.

On the night of 15th October the Admiralty once more affirmed that H.M.S. *Ark Royal* had not been sunk or damaged in any way. They repeated the announcement on the following day, but on 30th October H. W. Lascelles wrote to *The Times* from Denmark reporting the deep impression made in that country by Goebbels' propaganda, with particular reference to the *Ark Royal*.

The ship in question knew nothing of all this, for out on the blue wastes of the South Atlantic there were no papers and no mail from home. They were better off without such news, which could only have added to their frustration at not being able to hit back and prove their identity.

On 21st October the crew of the Norwegian s.s. *Lorentz W. Hansen* were landed at Kirkwall in the Orkneys, and reported that their ship had been sunk by a pocket battleship on the 14th. Their information confirmed the suspicion that there was more than one raider at large. On 22nd October the *Llanstephen Castle* picked up distress signals from the s.s. *Trevanion* and passed them on to the C.-in-C. at Freetown. Admiral Lyon at once ordered intensified searches to be made, but these produced no result.

The days wore on with no further sign from the enemy. The hunting warships relied a great deal upon the raiders' victims being able to make wireless signals before they were put out of action. Even these could not be relied upon, however. The *Trevanion* SOS, for example, could easily have been faked. As for her attacker, she could well have been an armed merchant cruiser. The forces which had sunk the *Clement* and the *Stonegate* on 5th October might have returned to Germany by now. It was very baffling and the German captains were helping to make it so by their cunning and resourcefulness. Whoever they were, they were well aware that they were being hunted by a large pack and were determined not to stay in any one spot too long, but to use the vast wilderness of the oceans to best advantage.

Meanwhile some smaller fish fell into the hunters' net. On 5th November *Ark Royal* and her escorting destroyers intercepted the steamer *Uhenfels*, which was carrying a cargo of hides, nuts, and copra, and a load of opium worth £250,000. She was at once shepherded into Freetown – another German merchantman which had failed to beat the blockade.

Then, on 8th November, the Admiralty learned the full story of their encounters from the masters of the *Clement* and *Stonegate*. What they had to tell definitely established the fact that two pocket battleships had been operating in the Atlantic. From their descriptions it looked as if the *Scheer* had sunk the *Clement*, and the *Deutschland* the *Stonegate*.

And now both ships had vanished again. But on 15th

November one of them was heard from – in the Indian Ocean. This raider sank a small tanker, the s.s. *Africa Shell*, in the Mozambique Channel, and the following day stopped a Dutch ship in the same area.

By this time the general run of German raiding strategy was becoming predictable. At least it seemed possible that the ship which had sunk the *Africa Shell* in the Indian Ocean might decide to double back into the South Atlantic again to confuse the pursuit and further its purpose. Accordingly, *Ark Royal* and *Renown* of Force K and *Sussex* and *Shropshire* of Force H were ordered to patrol a line south of the Cape with the object of intercepting the German if our estimate of his intentions turned out to be correct. The two forces took up their stations but were severely hampered for days on end by thick fog which badly restricted visibility and prevented any patrols by aircraft.

The situation remained unsatisfactory and obscure. On 23rd November the armed merchant cruiser *Rawalpindi* was sunk while escorting a convoy between Iceland and the Faroes. Her assailant was not clearly seen but was assumed to be the *Deutschland*. After this there was silence again. The hunters continued doggedly with their weary search.

On 2nd December, however, things began to move. A South African bomber sighted the German liner *Watussi* south of Cape Point and signalled her position to Forces H and K.

The *Shropshire* was first on the scene and picked up the liner's passengers and crew. Then Force K arrived to find *Watussi* scuttled and burning on the water. *Ark Royal* tried to finish her off with gunfire, but was still trying ineffectively to give her the *coup de grâce* when *Renown* signalled.

'Now let a gunnery ship have a go!'

This was a hit at Captain Power, who had been captain of H.M.S. *Excellent*, home of Royal Navy gunnery. But *Renown* made it good. Using only her foremost

65

turret she steamed slowly past the burning hulk and very soon sent her, hissing and steaming, to the bottom.

The same day brought more dramatic moves. The s.s. *Doric Star* sent out a distress message that he was being attacked by a German raider in a position between the Cape and Freetown, just south of St Helena. It looked as if the Indian Ocean raider had got clean through our southern patrol and resumed business in his old hunting ground.

Admiral Lyon immediately altered the dispositions of his ships. Force H was stationed so as to cover the trade route from the Cape to St Helena, and Force K was sent to sweep from the Cape to a position 28°S 15°W before going into Freetown.

Before they left on this sweep Force K put into Capetown to refuel, and the ships' companies had a few precious hours ashore, a blessed relief after all those miles of Admiralty weather. South Africa, sunny and smiling, was the first bit of civilisation they had seen since they left Scotland early in October. The *Ark Royal* was the centre of interest for the whole of Capetown. Here was concrete proof of German lies. Thousands of people flocked to see her, and it seemed as if all South Africa wanted to come and finger the gilt letters of her name to reassure themselves that the British Navy was still afloat after all. Cars came to the gangway in an endless stream, their owners anxious to take some *Ark Royal* man home with them for an hour or two before the ships were off again. At dawn next day Force K was only a pennant of smoke on the far horizon.

The cornerstones of Admiral Lyon's scattered fleet were Force K, Force H and Commodore Harwood's Force G. If the raider were finally cornered it seemed likely that one of these three groups would do it.

The composition of Harwood's squadron was varied from time to time. Overall, he could draw on the services of the heavy cruisers *Exeter* and *Cumberland* and the light cruisers *Ajax* and *Achilles*. With various combinations of these ships he continued to cover the trade route between Rio and the River Plate and at the same time keep a watch on German merchantmen in the neutral ports along the South American coast, in case they should break for home. At the beginning of December *Exeter* and *Cumberland* were at Port Stanley in the Falklands, *Achilles* was patrolling off Rio, and *Ajax* was on passage to the Plate from Port Stanley.

On 2nd December came the sinking of the *Doric Star* and the realisation that the raider was in the central South Atlantic. Force K was ordered to take up a central position whence it could go to Rio, to Freetown or to the Falklands to refuel before chasing the raider, whichever of those quarters turned out to be the likely one.

The men of *Ark Royal, Renown,* and their escorting destroyers were keyed up in expectation of a battle with the *Scheer*, especially the carrier's Swordfish pilots, who looked forward to making history by sighting and attacking a capital ship at sea.

Three thousand miles away from the spot where the *Doric Star* was sunk, Commodore Harwood had weighed the situation up and decided to concentrate his scattered ships. It was his guess that the raider would make for the South American coast, tempted by the rich traffic on the Plate–Rio route. He calculated that the ship which had sunk the *Doric Star* would be able to make Rio by 12th December or the Plate by the 13th. He himself lay off the Plate in the *Ajax*, with *Exeter* and *Cumberland* making all haste to leave Port Stanley and *Achilles* coming in from Rio. *Cumberland* could not be moved for the present, but by 6 p.m. on 12th December the other three ships were together off the entrance to the Plate.

Twenty-four hours later, at eight minutes past six on the morning of the 13th, *Ajax* reported smoke to the north-west. Eight minutes later *Exeter* signalled.

'I think it is a pocket battleship.'

Soon the four ships were hotly engaged. On receipt

67

of the news the C.-in-C. at Freetown ordered the *Dorsetshire* from the Cape and *Ark Royal*, *Renown*, and the cruiser *Neptune*, which had been patrolling to the north, to the scene of action.

Meanwhile the first phase of the battle was over. With his three lighter ships Commodore Harwood had engaged the eleven-inch guns of the pocket battleship, disposing his ships so as to divide the fire of the enemy. Before long the raider concentrated her main armament upon the *Exeter*, which was forced to retire from the fight badly damaged. Had the German been able to continue the pressure the eight-inch cruiser must surely have been sunk, but the raider was so badly hit herself that she put in to the neutral sanctuary of the Plate, leaving the *Achilles*, a disabled *Exeter*, and *Ajax*, with two of her turrets out of action, waiting for her outside.

This battered squadron was in no fit state to contain the pocket battleship. But Captain Langsdorff of the *Graf Spee*, as we now knew her to be, did not know what other units might by this time be near at hand. To sail or not to sail? He had twenty-four hours in which to effect repairs and make up his mind. At the end of that time he must either put to sea and face whatever opposition might have collected there, or be interned.

Our ships were on their way, *Dorsetshire* from the Cape, *Shropshire* in her wake, *Cumberland* from Port Stanley, Force K from the central South Atlantic.

On 15th December the gunnery officer of the *Graf Spee* told Captain Langsdorff that he could see the masts of the *Renown* from *Spee*'s control tower. Langsdorff at once concluded that both the battlecruiser and the *Ark Royal* were lying in wait for him. He managed to obtain a seventy-two hour extension of his stay in the neutral harbour. Then he cabled to Germany,

'Strategic position off Montevideo: Besides the cruisers and destroyers, *Ark Royal* and *Renown*. Close blockade at night. Escape into open sea and break through to home waters impossible.'

The day of 17th December dawned. At 8 p.m. the *Graf Spee*'s extension was due to expire. Mr Churchill, who had been following the battle closely from the Admiralty War Room, cabled to Mr Chamberlain, then on a visit to the Army in France,

'If the *Spee* breaks out, as she may do tonight, we hope to renew the action of the 13th with the *Cumberland*, an *eight* eight-inch gun ship, in place of the six-gun *Exeter* . . .'

The gunnery officer of the *Spee* must have been bad at warship identification if he could mistake the *Cumberland* for the *Renown*, for at the time when he reported the presence of the battlecruiser to Captain Langsdorff she and *Ark Royal* were still in mid-ocean, heading for Rio to refuel. They did not reach Rio until 17th December, and it was estimated that we should not be able to assemble any decisive weight of numbers at the mouth of the Plate until the 19th. However, as Mr Churchill said later, ' . . . we succeeded in creating the impression that they (*Ark Royal* and *Renown*) had already left Rio and were approaching Montevideo at thirty knots.'

But Captain Langsdorff believed that they were already there. The clerks in the German Embassy at Rio could have told him better, although they refused to believe their eyes. It must be another carrier, they insisted, with her name altered. Aboard the *Ark Royal* they had heard a lot about the famous *Flying Dutchman*, which was supposed to haunt the South Atlantic, and some of the people on the bridge actually claim to have seen the ghostly vessel. But to those Germans in Rio *Ark Royal* herself was the *Flying Dutchman* – modern dress.

She certainly bewitched Langsdorff and Hitler. The belief that she and *Renown* were near the Plate was enough. At 8.45 on the night of 17th December the *Ajax*'s seaplane radioed,

'*Graf Spee* has blown herself up.'

When this happened Force K was still a thousand

miles away, steaming south from Rio at full speed.

It was the end of the road for one German raider. Three days after he had sunk his ship Captain Langsdorff shot himself. Mr Churchill was now able to tell the First Sea Lord,

'Now that the South Atlantic is practically clear except for the *Altmark*, it seems of high importance to bring home the *Renown* and *Ark Royal* together with at least one of the eight-inch-gun cruisers. This will give us more easement in convoy work and enable refits and leave to be accomplished. . . . '

And so the *Ark* got her marching orders once more. But before she went home she had the proud task of escorting *Exeter* and *Ajax* to Freetown. *Exeter* had patched up her scars and she made light of them, but she was a proud ship. She it was who had borne the full force of those eleven-inch guns. How the *Ark* cheered her as she passed by! Later, Ark Royal Productions put on a special concert in her honour, run this time entirely by ratings. And *Ajax* too was cheered to the echo. How splendidly she had fought, this gallant lightweight, along with her New Zealand comrade *Achilles*! Leading-Seaman Cyril Calder aboard the *Ark* watched his old ship pass with a glow of pride and a lump in his throat; for this was one moment when he could have wished himself elsewhere – across that narrow lane of blue sea in the lovely ship he had known on that sunny first commission in the spacious days of peace and showing the flag.

The feelings of those aboard the *Ark Royal* were a mixture of pride, disappointment, frustration, and relief. The pilots were naturally cast down when they thought of that fog in the South Atlantic which had perhaps prevented the *Graf Spee* from falling a victim to their torpedoes. Now it was only 'might have been'. But they had the satisfaction of knowing that theirs had been an indispensible part of the whole difficult operation which had finally trapped the raider. In fact it had been mainly fear of the *Ark Royal* which had caused the Germans to decide that a break-through was impossible. Everybody on board the *Ark* knew this, and Vice-Admiral Wells was so jubilant when he realised it that he did a little dance on the spot.

During the search the Swordfish had flown nearly five million miles over that vast wasteland of ocean. However, if anyone could claim frustration it was the fighters, for they had had nothing to do at all. Meanwhile they all celebrated a tropical Christmas in Freetown, with free beer and cigars as a present from the people of Capetown. A store ship had arrived, too, and they had the benefit of her cargo. On Christmas morning in the blazing heat they held a fancy dress parade on the flight-deck, and the captain made the traditional rounds of the messdecks, which were gaily decked out with bright bunting and palm leaves.

The ship had crossed the Equator several times during the hunt for the *Spee*, but there had been no chance of celebrating in the customary way. *Ark*, however, was not the sort of ship to miss a chance of fun like that, and in Freetown Father Neptune's will was at last served. There had been a song in one of the Ark Royal Productions in which Bob Everett, made up to look like Captain Power, had sung 'I'm a captain who has never crossed the Line!' Everett had been very doubtful about the wisdom of pulling the captain's leg in this way, but Commander Eccles had assured him, having heard the song through and laughed heartily himself, that the captain would love it. So he did, and it was strange, but true, that he had never been initiated. He appeared for the occasion dressed in a shirt and a pair of shorts, and was lathered, 'shaved' and most soundly ducked. Few of those present ever forgot the sight of the captain being christened by the full impact of the jet from a power hose.

Then it was time to leave for England. The Germans knew very well that *Ark Royal* and *Renown* were expected home. By 10th February three U-boats had arrived in the South-Western Approaches with the special mission of attacking the two ships on their way home. They missed the speedy veterans, but managed to sink nine merchantment as a consolation prize.

The *Ark* arrived at Gladstone Dock in Liverpool on 15th February. The aircraft flew off at sea before she docked, and as soon as the last wire was ashore liberty men were sent to clean into number ones for the first time in many long, weary months. One watch then went off on seven days' leave.

Those left behind on the ship had to listen to Haw-Haw. By now he appeared to have accepted the fact that the *Ark* had risen from the dead, but was now telling the world that the Luftwaffe well knew where the carrier was and would soon be paying Liverpool a visit. In due course they came as he had promised and began their beastly work of destruction, although they never hit the carrier.

While the duty watch awaited their turn for leave, Chef John Coward, like many others, decided to bring his wife up to Liverpool. Her train arrived in the middle of an air-raid, hours late. Lime Street Station was blacked out as it steamed slowly in. John hurried down the darkened platform calling out his wife's name. At last he found her.

'Look!' she said. 'I fell out of the train and ruined a brand-new pair of nylons!'

It really was nice to be home again.

CHAPTER V

THE MIDNIGHT SUN

THE *Ark Royal* had barely finished her overhaul in Liverpool when she was at sea again hunting German shipping. In February 1940 the Commander-in-Chief, Western Approaches, learned that six German merchantmen lying in Vigo were about to try to break through to Germany, and he sent forces to intercept them. The Home Fleet lent him a squadron of fast ships, *Renown*, *Ark Royal*, the cruiser *Galatea*, and some destroyers, to help in the chase, and other groups including French warships and aircraft of Coastal Command joined in. The interception was very successful, and all but one of the ships were captured or sunk.

On 22nd March *Ark Royal* sailed from Portsmouth for the Mediterranean with three new Swordfish squadrons to work up night flying over the desert, practising in the cold darkness over a sea of sand what they would later do over the ocean itself.

Many of the pilots were new to the ship, and there was a new senior engineer, Lieutenant-Commander Tony Oliver, who would be a very important man in *Ark*'s flying activities, as part of his job made him responsible for all the flight-deck machinery. In this respect he had the safety of the aircrews in his hands.

He joined the ship at Portsmouth while she was having her degaussing gear fitted – a great belt of electric cable fitted round the ship inside her hull at water level to explode magnetic mines before they could blow up the ship. The gear was being fitted by the electrical branch, supervised, to everyone's amusement, by an officer with such a loud voice that he seemed to be able to make himself heard anywhere in the ship from where he stood. He was christened Baron de Gauss. Later in the war, when the Baron's ship was sunk by an *acoustic* mine, he himself was the first to admit that he must have brought it upon himself.

The *Ark* had always had her quota of Royal Air Force maintenance men, for the training from scratch of naval squadron ground-crews were inevitably taking time. The R.A.F. had generously lent many experienced mechanics to the Navy to train the new naval mainten-ance ratings and fill their places in the naval squadrons until the trainees were ready for operational service. They also allowed some men to transfer to the Navy. As late as December 1940 there were some two thousand R.A.F. officers and men still serving with the Navy.

Ted Eustance had had an interesting life in the R.A.F. In March 1938, with the international situation growing worse by the hour, the Air Force was hastily posting men all over the world to its strategically placed air stations. When L.A.C. Eustance's name came up the choice happened to be between a five-year tour overseas in an R.A.F. command, or a full commission of two and a half years with the Fleet Air Arm. Records took a pin and it landed on the latter. Ted was posted to the battle-ship *Barham* as member of her catapult flight.

It was a wet, dull day when he joined her in Ports-mouth Dockyard. The battleship was in C Lock at the time, undergoing a refit so as to be ready for war, and

74

everything was being done at high speed. As Ted climbed the steep gangway he was stunned by a big tea-chest swung clumsily round by a matelot as he tried to avoid the R.A.F. man. Ted was wearing gumboots and was hard put to keep his balance on the greasy metal deck. He felt completely lost.

There was a big conference in progress on the cata-pult turret and there were all kinds of dockyard engineers, ship's engineers, and gold braid awaiting the arrival of the Swordfish seaplane that the turret flight had already been preparing. To get to the catapult Ted had to climb over all kinds of lockers and up a metal ladder, then step across the wide gap between the outer guardshield of the huge 15-inch gun-turret, up the ladder and on to the turret top. He just couldn't keep his feet on the wet, oily metal, and when the aircraft was lifted on to the catapult cradle they had to climb on to the mass of girders that formed the catapult and guide the floatplane on to the catapult's securing spools. Ted, in his gumboots, kept slipping and sliding awkwardly. If he should miss his footing he would fall forty feet to the quarterdeck.

This was his place of work every day for the next two and a half years. Everything was utterly strange and be-wildering after R.A.F. life – the noise and clatter of drill-ing, welding and riveting on all sides, the tangle of cables and pipelines everywhere, the hundreds of stanchions, manholes, and steep, slippery metal hatches to negotiate, not to mention the strange names of authority – 'the Crusher', 'the Jaunty', 'the Buffer', 'Jimmy', 'bootnecks', 'Jack Dusty', 'Pusser', etcetera.

It was very bewildering to a L.A.C. engine fitter, whose only nautical knowledge had been acquired on the Liverpool-New Brighton ferry. The pipes, too, were fan-tastic: 'Out pipes!', 'Clean out and stow away spit-kids!', 'Up spirits!', ' 'Ands of the mess for spuds!', 'All the 'ands, 'eave-o, 'eave-o, 'eave-o; lash up and stow! Rise and shine, the mornin's fine, the sun's scorchin' yer bleedin' eyeballs!'

Still feeling lost on this their first day in the Royal Navy, Ted, the corporal rigger, the wireless and electrical mechanic, and the armourer wandered round this great fighting monster, blundering into forbidden quarters guarded by burnished marine guards, and bumping into awesome figures covered in gold braid who frowned at them in a way that made them tremble. They went on banging their heads and their shins on bulkheads and being shouted at by seamen petty officers until eventually they located their little store, which the sailors called a 'caboosh', shut the door and sank on to the bench to recover.

Such was a Royal Air Force man's first experience of the Navy. But gradually Ted grew used to it all. He found out that their seaplane cranedriver was an old friend from home, now a leading hand. He initiated Ted into Navy ways, although there were awkward moments like clambering along the boom and down into the crash boat, loaded with tools, which sorely tried him.

Barham cruised in the Mediterranean throughout 1938. She arrived at Naples on a friendly visit on the very day Mussolini chose to invade Albania. They left rather hurriedly and made contact with the fleet, with everyone busy fusing shell.

In August 1939 they were based on Alexandria. This was a worry for Ted, as his wife was away in Malta expecting her first baby. The only news he could get from Malta was of the evacuation of service wives and families. Ted was worried to death by now and appealed to the ship's padre for help.

A little later the padre piped for him. Ted was the father of a bouncing baby girl – one of the first war babies. They 'wet the baby's head' with wardroom whisky and arranged to have her christened on board when they reached Malta.

The christening eventually took place while *Barham* was alongside the dockyard wall in Grand Harbour. A picket boat collected the Eustance family and took them across the harbour to the ship.

A naval christening is always very thorough, and that of Ted's daughter was no exception. The water used was clean sea water, especially brought from outside the harbour breakwater, and the font was the upturned ship's bell. The ship's choir and a very large congregation were present to see a Royal Air Force daughter christened that day 'in the parish of Malta Dockyard'. Then they sailed, with Ted's wife a lonely figure on the breakwater to wave them off.

The war began to touch them now. At Gibraltar they joined the French battleship *Dunkerque* and waited at readiness while the *Graf Spee* chase was on in the South Atlantic. Then, when the German raider scuttled herself, they sailed for the United Kingdom to take part in operations in northern waters, escorted by the destroyers *Dainty*, *Diana*, and *Duchess*.

When they entered the Clyde there occurred one of those terrible tragic accidents which war always brings in its train. As they groped their way up-river at three in the morning in the pitch darkness of a wartime winter there was a sudden great jarring crash, then a violent shuddering as *Barham* went full astern.

Diving out of their hammocks they saw, in the light of searchlights, what looked like a submarine with a few men clinging on to her.

Then they realised that it was the upturned hull of the *Duchess*. *Barham* had rammed and overturned her. One or two of her scuttles were still above the water-line and Ted could see men trying vainly to climb out of the small openings. . . .

Most of her ship's company were trapped as she overturned, and only twenty-three survived out of a hundred and forty, in spite of every effort by *Barham*'s men, many of whom utterly exhausted themselves diving in again and again to look for signs of life in that black, chill water. It was a sight none of them ever forgot.

Barham served her time on the Arctic Patrol and was returning to port in company with the *Repulse* on 28th December when there was a tremendous explosion and a great deluge of water. The battleship began to list heavily. They had been torpedoed. Mercifully they did not go down, but limped into Liverpool two days later, very low in the water, with several compartments flooded and a gaping hole below the water-line.

This episode was one of Mr Churchill's best-kept secrets of the war, and Ted Eustance got into trouble when he was at Lee-on-Solent immediately afterwards waiting for *Barham*'s seaplane 'Mitzi' to arrive, by imperilling security in asking after her whereabouts.

Mrs Eustance managed to get an air passage home from Malta. After they had been together at Lee for a few happy days, Ted awoke one morning to see the *Ark Royal* in the Solent. At eleven the same morning he was told to be on his way by the 1.20 train from Portsmouth bound for Hatston, the naval aerodrome at Scapa Flow.

He arrived during an air-raid, which was now a regular thing at Scapa. Hitler had invaded Scandinavia, and the Luftwaffe was in Denmark and southern Norway. Heinkels from Stavanger could now bomb our home bases as well as our expeditionary force in Norway and our ships at sea with much greater ease.

But they were having their work cut out, in spite of greater numbers and better organisation, in overcoming Norway. Allied ships and Fleet Air Arm aircraft flying from the carriers and from the Orkneys were preventing the Germans from landing further troops and supplies by sea in central and northern Norway.

When Ted Eustance arrived in Scapa he joined 803 Skua Squadron at Hatston. This squadron, under Lieutenant-Commander Lucy, was working with 800 Squadron in attacks on German shipping and aircraft in Norwegian waters. Very early in the campaign they sank the cruiser *Koenigsburg* in Bergen Harbour in a daring dive-bombing attack. Then *Glorious* and *Ark Royal* arrived in Scapa Flow, hotfoot from the Mediterranean. The two carriers left at once and headed for Norway, taking the Skuas from Hatston with them. It was 23rd April.

Allied troops and ships were fighting bitterly in Norway and in the fiords and coastal waters against massive German strength. In fact the Germans were beating us all along the line, and the situation had become desperate. They were better prepared and better equipped, and they had thrust into Denmark and on through Norway with tremendous force, helped enormously by the fifth column in both countries. They beat us decisively to the punch in the race to occupy Norway with its enormous advantages in the shape of advance bases and, most of all, of the Swedish iron ore which had been flowing south to Germany via Narvik in northern Norway.

The Germans swiftly crossed the Skagerrak and took Oslo, the Norwegian capital. Then Kristiansand, Bergen, Trondheim, Narvik, and the excellent air-base at Stavanger fell to them and were taken over before we could do anything to stop them. The Luftwaffe promptly moved in and soon had four hundred bombers in the air.

We counter-attacked with the meagre forces we had, of which only the Royal Navy outmatched the Germans.

Our destroyers, led by *Warspite*, smashed the German destroyer force which had taken troops to Narvik in a spirited action in the fiords around Narvik and bottled up the German garrison there. Then came the task of landing a small Allied expeditionary force in central Norway to try and stop the Germans who were advancing rapidly northwards on Trondheim.

We had about as much chance of doing that as the Old Contemptibles had had of smashing Kaiser Bill. To begin with we had no real idea of how to land a modern army from the sea. A few enthusiasts before the war had done what they could, but they were not encouraged or supported enough by authority, and the idea of combined operations was still sucking on the bottle.

But somehow we got over the handicap of having the wrong equipment and the wrong units in the wrong ships at the wrong time heading for the wrong place with no properly designed landing-craft to put them ashore when they got there, and eventually blundered into Norway. A small force went in at Namsos to the north-east, and another at Aandalsnes to the south-west, with the idea of converging on Trondheim.

It was the vaguest and most forlorn of hopes. The Germans had a thousand bombers and fighters on the spot and we had none, nor could we hope for any. And we had no airfields to fly from in any case. The Germans had thought of this and began using frozen lakes as air-strips from the beginning. We made a feeble attempt to copy them when it was too late to do any good.

Naturally the Luftwaffe bombed the allied troops ashore severely and there seemed to be no stopping them. About all we had was courage, and that is never enough. It only makes the loss of fine men more shameful and the blundering of brass hats and politicians more despicable.

Alone the *Furious* did what she could to protect our men ashore with air cover. But what could a few fighters do against a horde? Even they could not fly all the time for they met some very bad weather during much of that terrible fortnight. Every time the Fleet Air Arm machines went up they set about and knocked down enemy machines against odds of ten to one. They were wonderful, but they were so few, and the old *Furious* almost burned herself out with the tremendous pressure. Her old machinery badly needed rest and repair.

But *Ark Royal* and *Glorious* came full speed from Scapa and packed her off home to refit. They had brought with them the finest air group in the world – superb and expendable. It was now that the 'pit ponies' came up from *Ark*'s lower hangar and fought like the thoroughbreds they were.

Their brief was to protect our ships and our troops at the landing places, and attack German air-bases. Between them the two carriers had four fighter squadrons and four bomber squadrons to do the job, all of them made up of slow and obsolete machines. The Skuas and Swordfish had to face the latest modern land-based fighters. To shoot down Me.109's you needed Hurricanes and Spitfires.

Where were they? They were all in France and England – fighting desperately against the great blitzkrieg which Hitler had now unleashed against France and the Low Countries, and preparing to defend the very shores of Britain herself.

And in any case, land-based fighters and ship-borne fighters were different animals, and, according to the fuddy-duddies, would always be so. We had no airfields in Norway, only floating ones fighting the heavy weather at sea. And of course the idea of flying a Hurricane from those was fantastic. . . .

So here were the Skuas, and there were the 109's – and the foul, filthy weather.

The day after *Ark Royal*'s arrival in Norwegian waters they went up and fought off the Messerschmitts and Heinkels and screaming Stukas over Namsos and Aandalsnes, where the Nazis were wrecking and burning everything and slaughtering our defenceless soldiers and the men in the few anti-aircraft cruisers, trawlers, and destroyers, who were in the fiords on a suicide mission.

The Skuas flew and fought with unbelievable thrust and courage. They were outnumbered, but in every other way they were superior. They outflew and outmanoeuvred the Germans every time, and showed those bullies how to fight. They shot down at least twenty Nazis and badly hurt twenty more. And, more than that, they so scared the life out of the others that they began to hide in the clouds if the odds were less than six to one in their favour.

On 27th April five Skuas attacked two Junkers 88's dive-bombing a British convoy entering harbour. The Germans both burst into flames and fell away towards

6   81

the sea. The Skuas switched their attack then to a bunch of Heinkels and set two of these on fire. All the time more and more German aircraft were to be seen heading for the convoy. Two Dornier 17's came in to try their luck and were very swiftly dealt with by the naval pilots. These were followed by a scattered formation of fifteen Heinkels. Some of the Skuas were out of ammunition by now, and the last one just had enough rounds in his guns to shoot down one of the Heinkels. Then he joined the rest, who were pursuing the rather hair-raising tactics of head-on mock attacks, bluffing the enemy into breaking off and dropping their bombs haphazard, routing them by sheer will power. . . .

The Germans, for their part, had only managed to destroy one Skua so far, but, tragically, eight others had run out of fuel before they could reach the carriers and had been swallowed up by the sea.

The Swordfish fought a hero's battle too. In fog, in bitter cold, and against the fast fighters of the Luftwaffe, they went up and did a superlative job of work.

Bob Everett smelled smoke from the enemy for the first time when he went into a fiord to look for the frigate *Black Swan*. 'You go in there and pass *Black Swan* the new code,' he was ordered. On their way up the fiord they met up with some British destroyers. The destroyers had been bombed all day and were in a mood to let loose at anything that came too close. Digger Gerrett in the back seat fired what he thought was going to be the Very light signal which would establish their friendly intentions. Unfortunately the pistol produced instead a brown smoke puff. The destroyers saw it and thought it was flak and let fly at the Swordfish. 'I hurried down to the sea in my Stringbag,' said Everett afterwards, 'and put him right.'

They then went about their mission and dropped their message for *Black Swan* in a bag at the side of the fiord for a boat from the ship to collect. Everett was so excited when he returned to the *Ark* that he missed all the arrester wires and ended up in the barrier.

He reported to the bridge and told them what had happened. 'Good!' said the captain. 'Gunsmoke! Nothing like it!'

Usually their orders were vague, mainly owing to the confusion of the fighting. They would be told simply to load their aircraft with a mixed bag of disruptives and 'explosive stores', fly up the fiords and bomb anything hostile. The Stringbags, meant for torpedo attacks on ships, not bombing raids on heavily defended shore targets, were nevertheless sent in on one occasion to bomb Vaernes aerodrom while the Skuas attacked German ships and seaplanes in Trondheim harbour, close by. Coming in in broad daylight from a height of six thousand feet through flak 'so close you could smell it', as one pilot said, the Swordfish shattered all the hangars and many of the buildings and aircraft on the field.

The elderly biplanes always operated with an umbrella of enemy fighters, who would make frantic passes at the old ladies, unable to believe that these tottering symbols of British decadence could outfly them and avoid their bullets. Sometimes the Swordfish did this by using slick aerobatics to avoid the fast all-or-nothing attacks of the very much faster German machines, side-slipping or banking sharply at the last moment and making the 109's miss. Sometimes they would use the topography of fiord and mountain to lure their lunging attackers into one-way streets among the snow-clad cliffs where speed was a death-trap and only a wily old hand could survive.

'Delayed by three Messerschmitts,' or some such laconic message they would signal to the ship, as if in the last stages of boredom, then amble on board later, shot full of holes. Sometimes they did not get back.

Often aircrews would return to the land of the living long after they had been given up for lost with an incredible tale to tell. One young midshipman pilot was forced to land through lack of fuel on a frozen lake next to a crashed R.A.F. Gladiator fighter. It seemed the most natural thing in the world to him to transfer the petrol from the Gladiator to his own Skua, take off again and fly back three hundred and fifty miles to Shetland. He was alone in the aircraft, with no observer to navigate for him, but he made his landfall with no trouble.

'How on earth did you find your way?' he was asked.

'Well, it sounds a bit of a line,' he said, self-consciously, 'but actually I borrowed an atlas from a Norwegian kid and, er, used that.'

Another routine fighter patrol from the *Ark* had a most unusual outcome for one Skua crew.

Over Aandalsnes they met a Heinkel and shot him down, only to force land a moment later themselves with a shot-up engine.

The observer gathered up his precious navigation instruments and confidential books from the rear cockpit and they set fire to the machine. Then they set off to struggle through the deep snow towards a hut they had seen on the hillside. The hut was empty so they made themselves at home and tried to start a fire. The observer said later in his official account of the incident,

'We did manage to get some sort of blaze going, and I suppose we must have been there about fifteen or twenty minutes when we heard a whistle outside. Somewhat startled, because we thought there was no-one else within miles of us, we rushed to the door, Birdie leading.

'To our amazement we saw five or six Huns dressed in flying-clothes coming up the last few hundred yards of the hill towards our hut. The first one, who had just blown his whistle, was carrying a revolver, and as far as we could see all the rest had some sort of weapon. We, on the contrary, possessed between us one pocket knife.

'Something had to be done, and Birdie did it. After only a few moments' hesitation he stepped out of the doorway and shouted, "Do any of you speak English?"

'I think the Huns must have been just about as surprised as we were ourselves. At any rate, after a slight pause the leader shouted back that he could speak English. By this time they were all collected in a bunch about twenty yards away and all had drawn their revolvers. This did not seem to deter Birdie in the least. He simply shouted "Come here! You are my prisoners!"

'There was a most painful silence which seemed to last for years. Then they all stepped forward and held their hands up.

'It had worked; and now, having got our prisoners, we had to decide what to do with them. After a number of questions and answers in broken English, we discovered that the Huns were the crew of our Heinkel.'

It was a strange and tense situation, and only the British pair saw the humour of it as well. However, they managed to keep the Germans submissive and the following day a party of Norwegians found them. The observer takes up his story again,

'There were only four Norwegians and they had divided themselves into two pairs, one in front of the house and the other going round behind. When they saw me they motioned me forward, and indicated that my hands should go up as well. . . . The other two routed out the rest of the Heinkel crew, and we were all paraded in a line with our hands up. Birdie and I did out best to tell the Norwegians that we were British, but although they could speak a sort of English, they were not prepared to accept our word without proof.

'The situation was tricky. They seemed to have an idea that we might have guns stuck in the tops of our flying-boots, and the fellow in front of me said, "Take off your boots." I lowered my hands to comply when a voice from behind me said, "Put up your hands!" As he accompanied this last order with a jab in the back from his rifle, I thought he deserved more attention, and so put my hands up again. This was greeted by a shout from the front that my boots must come off, and so in desperation I started to put my hands down again. The man at the back seemed quite infuriated by this and threatened that unless my hands did stay up he would shoot me. I think I might say that the situation had now grown rather more than tricky. I know I didn't like it a bit.

'Then Birdie had an idea, and between us we tried every dialect and language known to us both, from "Look 'ere, old cock" to "Bai Jove, old man!" including schoolboy French and Spanish. But all to no effect.

'Then I had a brilliant idea. I quickly dropped my left hand, turned my breast pocket inside out, showing the tailor's label, and shouted,

'Look! "Gieves, London!"''

A few days later they struggled into Aandalsnes and made contact with our troops there.

Those who returned to the *Ark* always did so at the utmost extreme of weariness. 'It was cold, damp, and frightening,' said Everett later.

Sometimes the aircraft were used as a sort of human radar, in the absence of the real thing. The machines would fly out as far as they could without losing sight of the ship and keep an anti-aircraft watch with binoculars, the idea being that in the advent of a sudden air attack approaching the ship these planes could at least send a warning to her before they themselves were shot down ... It was very cheerless work, and the Swordfish crews, unlike the Skua men already warm inside their enclosed cockpits, still had no proper, lined flying-clothes.

And when the aircraft did return it was usually to run into an air attack upon the ship. She was heavily bombed all this time, though never hit, thanks to good gunners and brilliant ship handling – and the human radar! One day she was under attack by Heinkels and Junkers almost continuously for twelve hours, and deluged time and again with the spray from near misses. Her men began to swear that some sort of divine providence protected the ship. 'The luck of the *Ark Royal*', a catch-phrase which had begun with her narrow escapes earlier in the war, now became common, first in the *Ark* herself, then throughout the Navy, and finally in the popular imagination.

The men at her guns became slap-happy with action after endless hours at action stations, with only a break now and again for a corned dog sandwich and a gulp of hot cocoa to keep them going.

Once Jack Bishop stood on his gun platform and saw a Stuka flatten out at the end of its dive, wobbly and unstable, and fly right down the starboard side of the ship under her guns. Jack and the others stood at their guns and looked right down into the cockpit of the Nazi bomber as she rocked and roared by, unable to do anything else but stare as their guns would not depress to that degree.

Down in the engine-room and boiler-rooms it was difficult to estimate the danger. All explosions sounded very much the same, and it was impossible to tell which noise was a bomb exploding and which the racket of their own guns. But friends on deck did their best to keep them informed, and many a running commentary passed through a dozen stages of distortion before it reached a stoker or an engine-room artificer or Tony Oliver down in the eerie silence of the soundproof machinery control room, where there were only the dials and gauges to tell them what was happening to the ship.

By now the situation in central Norway was hopeless. Our men and their French and Norwegian allies had fought desperately their hopeless action, and the big battalions of air power had beaten them, helped generously by incompetence in high quarters. Once again in our history it was 'too little and too late'. British soldiers, sailors, and airmen had had to pay with their flesh and blood for the blind stupidity of politicians who had neglected to give them even a fraction of the air cover they needed so desperately. It would not be the last time, unfortunately, that the sins of the men who made the speeches and planned the battles would be visited upon the men who had to fight them.

Soon it became obvious that we must evacuate the Trondheim area. The Navy came and took the soldiers off. Cruisers, destroyers, trawlers, and transports picked them up under a sky full of bombers, plucking them from blazing jetties and out of shattered towns.

Overhead Royal Naval aircraft did what they could to protect the evacuation. *Ark Royal* sent her Skuas over the fiords again and again and suffered so many near misses from bombs herself that she definitely seemed to have a charmed life.

On May Day the ship was attacked particularly heavily. The Skuas shot down one of the enemy bombers and the guns damaged several more. By now she had done her work in the Trondheim offensive. The Allies had left the area and the Luftwaffe were bombing our expeditionary force in the Narvik area, three hundred and fifty miles further north.

Our forces there, working from their base at Harstad sixty miles away from Narvik across a network of fiords were trying to capture the iron-ore port itself, garrisoned by German troops, and deny it to the Germans. The débâcle at Namsos and Aandalsnes gave even greater importance to the campaign in the north. It was our only beachhead left in Norway.

In the early stages of the Narvik campaign the Luftwaffe had been too busy at Namsos to do more than send a few bombers up from Trondheim, which dropped men and supplies to their troops north of Narvik, across the other side of Ronbaks Fiord.

When Trondheim was cleared, however, they switched all their attention to Narvik. Their forces started moving north to relieve the beleaguered German garrison in Narvik town, and they began to use airfields farther up the coast from which to bomb our troops and ships in the fiords and ashore near Narvik. At the Harstad base the Allies were attacked throughout the night, and the cruisers and destroyers in the fiords were dive-bombed and hit continually, while the anti-submarine trawlers patrolling there lost half their number.

Once again it was a case for fighters. This time we had

learned a severe lesson and managed things a little better.

After her bad time on May Day *Ark Royal* went back to Scapa to refuel. On 4th May she sailed again for Norway, this time to give fighter protection over Narvik.

On the same day Wing-Commander Atcherley of Schneider Trophy fame flew out from Britain and took charge of the finding and development of aerodromes. We had to have landing strips for fighters, and we had to have them quickly. Lieutenant Franklin of the Fleet Air Arm had already made a start in organising the clearing of two snow-covered airstrips in the area, one near the village of Skaanland and another at Bardufoss high in the mountains north of Narvik. Bardufoss was the better of the two but would take longer to clear. Meanwhile all available labour was put to work at Skaanland to clear the three to four feet of snow away and level and drain the ground.

Meanwhile fighter cover was left to the *Ark Royal*'s Skuas. The ship cruised about a hundred miles off the coast and flew off fighters almost every day while *Glorious* and *Furious* waited at home to bring more fighters for the airfields ashore when they were ready. Urgent signals arrived at Harstad every day asking when that would be.

The handful of Skuas and their pilots and air-gunners were preposterously overworked during this desperate fortnight when the shovels flew night and day on snow-bound Skaanland and Bardufoss. It was quite impossible to satisfy all the calls on their services, but the *Ark* kept the air above the fiords patrolled regularly and fought tremendous odds every day. By now the German pilots had realised that the Fleet Air Arm men were tough opponents and they began to take things very much more seriously. They were using faster bombers now, the Heinkel Mark V's, which could outdistance the slow Skuas or dodge them in the clouds. But Vice-Admiral Wells, *Ark*'s own admiral, wrote, 'The performance of the aircraft crews was nevertheless as fine as ever.'

They certainly had a rough time. Lieutenant-

Commander Lucy, who had sunk the *Koenigsburg* and later joined the *Ark* with 803 Squadron, and his observer, Mike Hanson, were lost on one of the bad days.

In a wild tangle of head-on and stern attacks Skuas and Heinkels were mixing it over the fleet anchorage at 18,000 feet.

One Heinkel broke off and spiralled down on fire. Two others dived for the water. Lucy went down after them and put a burst into one of them, whose port engine started to pour out smoke.

The other Heinkel's returning fire hit the Skua as it was turning away and it exploded just above the sea. Later Lucy's body was picked up out of the water, although there was no trace of Hanson.

Meanwhile two more Skuas attacked two dive-bombing Ju 87's and shot one down into the sea. The Skuas watched five men struggle from the sinking plane and swim ashore.

During the Skuas' period of glory the Swordfish took on a variety of jobs. They patrolled the fiords and coastal waters looking for submarines, their pilots, observers, and air-gunners frozen and fed up in their open cockpits. It was better to have something definite to do, even photographing enemy positions ashore. That was hot work and concentrating on it warmed you up.

But the hottest work of all came when these wonderful old aeroplanes once more turned themselves into fighter-bombers and did a job which would have been given later in the war to Mosquitoes, Tempests and Hurri-bombers. They began to carve out quite a niche for themselves in the bombing of railway communications.

They had a good party on 9th May. The target was the railway east of Narvik which came up from German-held Norway. Ranged aboard *Ark*, they were airborne almost as soon as they opened the throttle, and once in the air they made for the target, battle against fierce headwinds all the way. The great cold gusts caught the light and airworthy biplanes like paper kites, and their gallant Pegasus engines had to fight doggedly to keep them on course. But they beat steadily to windward and eventually reached the rendezvous two hours late.

After all their efforts it was a good feeling to see Skuas from the old *Ark* overhead when they got there. Under this umbrella the Stringbags went down and blasted the railway. One wave hit a viaduct near the Swedish border, tearing up the track and skimming a stick of bombs into the mouth of a tunnel. The second wave bombed a station and overturned a train. They all returned to the *Ark* somehow, with flak scars all over them, one with a main-plane that looked like a shredded lettuce leaf. A destroyer returned the crew of one of the Skuas who had force-landed near Narvik and walked through the German lines back into the war.

All the time the *Ark Royal* kept up this constant pressure there was no rest for anybody. It was a round-the-clock offensive, for there was no darkness and flying went on ceaselessly under the midnight sun.

The strain fell more heavily on some than on others. The whole ship was more or less permanently at action stations and there was little or no time to stand down for a rest. But a gunner at least had some periods of inactivity.

But there were no such lulls in the engine-room. A man on watch down there always had something to attend to, and would be on the go all the time with no rest at all. After days and nights of almost continuous standing-to it was difficult to keep going. They just kept on, doing it for the old *Ark*, where 'purpose knows no rest.'

It was the same, if not worse, for the squadron ground-crews. A corporal fitter like Ted Eustance had to check daily the servicing of the engines and their installations for Blue Section of 803's Skuas, which had joined the ship at Scapa. This entailed refuelling, re-oiling, the periodic inspection of plugs, H.T. leads, magnetoes, oil and fuel filters and tanks, the repair and maintenance of propellers, the checking and replacement of valves and valve springs, the checking and alignment of all engine controls, the replacement of damaged or worn components such as magnetoes, carburetters, fuel and oil pumps, the checking of all oil and fuel pipes for leaks and replacing them whenever necessary – and that was often in these hectic operations – and the removal and installation of whole engines as well as the quick diagnosing and rectifying of all running defects.

Then Ted and another corporal had to take charge of the tail steering-arm whenever the aircraft were moved.

They were thus on duty whenever the machines were ranged on the lift to go up to the flight-deck or struck-down below again after landing. All movements had to be carried out on the double, with the mainplanes folded, in a confined space, and a mistake could be very dangerous.

The lift would descend, and 800 Squadron in the top hangar would push their aircraft on, with 803 doing the same below. When the lift went up again 800's machine was trundled off on to the flight-deck by the deck-landing party, and 800's hangar party took 803's Skua from the bottom hangar temporarily into the top hangar. When the lift descended again this machine was put on to the top lift-platform and sent up to the flight-deck, while the lower hangar party put another Skua on to the lower platform. The whole process was then repeated. There was fierce competition among the corporals to knock a few seconds off the record.

Battle and rough-weather damage made their job a constant, aching battle against the clock. And it did not always end there. Ted, as a corporal, had to supervise all the engine mechanics in his section of the squadron and take charge of a mess when off duty.

All this wearisome slogging was done against a background of roaring engines and the stink of oil and petrol and sweat down in the hangars, with the ship shuddering and heeling as she evaded the bombers or rolling and heaving in bad weather.

Ark's fighters, few in number, were making themselves felt. 'Despite the cloud and drizzle,' wrote Rear-Admiral L. E. H. Maund, at the time a captain in one of the naval vessels supporting the expeditionary force and one of the earliest enthusiasts for combined operations, 'we twice had the joy of seeing two flights of Skuas from the *Ark Royal* over us. Nothing but quite impossible weather would stop them.' He could not then know that he himself was destined to have a very much closer connection with the *Ark*.

During this phase the Skuas had destroyed or damaged six enemy machines, with nine more probables. The reverse side of the balance sheet showed nine Skuas lost and five Swordfish. Two men were killed and two slightly wounded. In the circumstances it was a fair score, saying much for the courage and even more for the skill of the aircrews themselves. But they could not go on alone indefinitely.

On 18th May *Glorious* and *Furious* arrived off the coast, their hangars full of aircraft. No. 710 Squadron of Royal Naval Walruses flew off to Harstad, where they turned themselves into bombers and performed all manner of energetic and foolhardy things for which they were never intended.

Still the airstrips ashore were not ready, and the two new arrivals steamed impatiently up and down off-shore, waiting to discharge the rest of their priceless cargo.

Then, on 21st May, No. 263 Gladiator Squadron flew ashore to Bardufoss from *Furious*. Sixteen machines landed on the runways flanked with snow, although two of them and a Swordfish crashed and had to be written off.

But relief had arrived, and *Ark Royal*, running low on fuel by now, was able to steam away to Scapa once more. *Glorious*, also short of fuel, left on 21st May after the last fighter had been flown off. Five days later, on 26th

May, *Glorious* returned, and about midnight the people of Harstad were immensely cheered when a squadron of R.A.F. Hurricanes flew in over their heads. One flight landed at Skaanland and the rest at Bardufoss.

'The change in outlook that came with the arrival of the fighters is difficult to describe,' wrote Admiral Maund. 'It was shared by troops, ships, and Norwegians. I was standing on the upper road of Harstad with the public gardens in front of me and a row of attractive wooden houses behind me as the Hurricanes roared past. I was joined by a Norwegian and his wife who came running out of a house nearby, and as the fighters passed by our faces were broad with smiles, and the wife, clapping her hands, shouted, "And now we will teach them – those bombers!"'

The new fighters took heavy toll of the enemy. German air strength was now very great, and on 27th May two of the Gladiators from *Furious* shot down four enemy aircraft over Bodo. Then the Hurricanes began operating as well, and within a fortnight forty-eight enemy bombers had fallen over Bodo and the fiords. Enemy sorties grew fewer and fewer.

But it was too late to do any lasting good. It was quite obvious by now that we could never hold Narvik with the slender forces at our disposal, and in any case all our strength was needed in France and England to stem the surging fury of the German blitzkrieg.

Narvik fell to the Allies on 28th May, but we only remained long enough to smash the town's iron-ore facilities, so as to render them inoperative for a time, before evacuating the area and thus our last foothold in Norway.

Among the last to leave were the Royal Air Force fighters, now greatly reduced in numbers, which had taken over from the Skuas of the *Ark* and done such magnificent work in the same tradition.

There was only one way of getting them off. They had to fly back aboard the carriers whence they had come.

But landing aboard a carrier is a very much more hazardous thing than taking off. These R.A.F. pilots had had no training at all in deck landing, but with naval help and encouragement they made the attempt.

The surviving Gladiators got aboard *Glorious* without much trouble. Then it was the turn of the Hurricanes, eight of them in number.

Fast monoplane fighters of the 300 m.p.h. class had never landed on carriers before, and it was commonly supposed that it could not be done. But No. 46 Squadron R.A.F. confounded the armchair experts. In his despatch, 'Norway Campaign, 1940', the British Naval C.-in-C., Admiral of the Fleet the Earl of Cork and Orrery, wrote, 'The courageous action of the pilots in volunteering to fly their machines on to the flying deck of *Glorious*, and of Group-Captain Moore in allowing it to be done, resulted in all eight being got safely away. . . . ' Aboard the *Ark*, which had returned to Norwegian waters on 2nd June, the R.A.F. men watched with service pride the Hurricanes land one by one aboard the other carrier. *Glorious* was short of fuel by now and was ordered to proceed independently to home waters. In the half-light she flashed *Ark Royal* a message, then steamed away with her two destroyers, *Acasta* and *Ardent*.

On 4th June the embarkation of the first contingent of 15,000 men in six transports and the *Vindictive* was begun. It was intended that the ships of the Home Fleet should come from home waters to escort them. On that morning the *Scharnhorst* and *Gneisenau*, with the heavy cruiser *Admiral Hipper*, and four destroyers, left Kiel, planning to attack our Harstad base on the night of 8th-9th June. They had no knowledge of our evacuation or of the dispositions of so many British ships.

On 7th June 10,000 more men began to embark in seven ships. The same day Admiral Marschall in the *Scharnhorst* received a report of two large groups of British ships. He decided to make for the southernmost group.

At 1 a.m. next day the first group of transports was met by ships of the Home Fleet. But only the *Valiant* and a few destroyers had arrived. *Repulse* and *Renown*, which should have come with them, had been diverted to chase two suspected enemy ships reported north-east of the Faroes heading for Iceland.

The embarkation was now complete. At Harstad Captain Maund walked slowly and sadly down to the jetty, where a motor boat took him out to the cruiser *Southampton*, which wore the flag of Lord Cork. Then they put to sea to pick up the second convoy of transports.

'As we approached Andenes Point,' wrote Maund, 'to shape our course out into the Atlantic, the first German aircraft came over to report what was happening and to bring the bombers on to the retiring convoy. It would not take long for an aircraft at 100 m.p.h. to catch us on our twelve-knot journey. Fortunately the *Ark Royal* was with us. . . . '

As well as *Ark Royal* and *Southampton*, the second convoy had the cruiser *Coventry* and eight destroyers. They steamed away from the Norwegian coast down the route which the *Glorious* had taken just before them.

On 8th June Admiral Marschall's squadron sank the *Oil Pioneer*, her escorting trawler *Juniper*, and the troopship *Orama*, which was returning empty to Britain. The hospital ship *Atlantis*, which was accompanying the others, was left unmolested. The German admiral reported his progress to his Group Command West. He was ordered to detach the *Hipper* and the destroyers to deal with the British convoys and proceed with *Scharnhorst* and *Gneisenau* to Harstad.

On the 9th *Hipper* and the destroyers were forced to return to Trondheim through lack of fuel. Admiral Marschall decided to ignore his orders and go for the bigger game which lay spread out before him at sea.

That same morning the *Valiant*, returning from escorting the first convoy in order to pick up the second, met the *Atlantis*, to learn from her of the presence of the German squadron. She at once hastened towards the second convoy, which was still four hundred miles away to the north of her. On the evening of 7th June Admiral J. H. D. Cunningham had left Tromso for Britain in the cruiser *Devonshire* with the King of Norway on board. That afternoon Admiral Cunningham picked up the faint ghost of a distress message. With the gravity of his own responsibility in mind he did not, however, dare to break radio silence to pass on the message.

Later that same afternoon the German radio broadcast a triumphant story. Making all speed for the convoy, *Scharnhorst* and *Gneisenau* had stumbled upon the *Glorious* and her two destroyers, and had sunk them all. Perhaps disorganised by her previous embarkation of the R.A.F. fighters, and with Hurricanes cluttering the flight-deck and hangars, the carrier was caught unawares at four in the afternoon. The German gunners were, as usual, deadly accurate, and their first hits wrecked the hangars, making it impossible to fly off a striking force. The destroyers laid a smoke screen but could not save the carrier, and at 5.20 she had to be abandoned, stopped and blazing. A few minutes later the *Ardent* was battered under, having fired her last torpedo at the enemy. At 5.40 *Glorious* turned over to starboard and sank. *Acasta*, alone now, steered for the enemy. With her last breath she fired a salvo of torpedoes and hit the *Scharnhorst* abaft her after turret. Then at 6.8 this gallant little fighting ship sank, shattered by the overwhelming weight of gunfire, leaving the German sailors deeply moved by her bravery.

When the news reached him Admiral Forbes at once left Scapa with *Rodney*, *Renown* (now recalled from her wild goose-chase to Iceland), and six destroyers, to pick up the returning convoy, ordering other ships to the scene as well. Ten thousand men were at sea in those ships and, only some hundred miles west of the position where *Glorious* had gone down, was the *Devonshire* with the King of Norway on board.

But the martyred ships had saved the others. With *Scharnhorst* badly damaged by *Acasta*'s torpedo, Admiral Marschall went into Trondheim later the same day. The convoy had had a narrow escape, for it had been routed down the path of the *Glorious*. As it was, the ships returned safely to home waters, although *Ark Royal* and the other convoy escorts had to fight off enemy bombers on the way.

On 11th June thirty-eight survivors from the *Glorious* and one from the *Acasta* were picked up by a Norwegian fishing boat.

Two days later units of the Home Fleet, including *Ark Royal*, left Scapa Flow and headed for Trondheim, where the German battlecruisers lay.

In the *Ark Royal* volunteers were called for from the aircrews. Every man came forward. Most of them had had friends on the *Glorious*. At midnight the *Ark* flew off sixteen Skuas, each armed with one five-hundred-pound bomb.

Just before they left Ned Finch-Noyes came into Bob Everett's cabin. The two pilots were very close friends now. Between them they had put on the Ark Royal Productions which had helped to keep the morale of *Ark Royal* so high.

Finch-Noyes said, 'I don't know if I'm going to come back from this one, Bob. I want you to give these personal things to my wife.'

The Skuas took off in appalling weather, but there was no question of their not going this time. One by one they rocked and roared down the deck and then were gone.

Those left aboard waited, tense and anxious. Time went slowly by. Then *Ark Royal* ran into dense fog. She could not slow down or alter course. The Skuas were somewhere above the fog, expecting their ship to be in a certain place at a certain time, and there she had to be.

The fog was so thick that Tony Oliver, standing on the starboard side of the flight-deck aft, could not see the island.

Still the ship forged on at twenty-seven knots through the fog.

They reached the rendezvous and waited. Presently they heard engines overhead.

They could not tell how many, but they all felt relief that the Skuas had returned, relief mixed with anxiety as to how they were to be guided safely down.

The machines could be heard circling for a while. Then they heard one engine close to the stern.

The engine note roared then faded. Tony Oliver saw a shape burst out of the mist over the roundown, to be grabbed swiftly by the arrester wires and wrenched to a stop.

One by one they came thrusting in through the fog. Every lunge at the deck was a tense moment for the watchers. They did not all get aboard on their first pass. Sometimes Oliver and the others round him would feel their hearts sink as a Skua plunged out of the fog only to surge past them up the deck and be swallowed up by the swirling greyness for'ard, its engine roaring as the pilot opened up to go round again.

The first pilots to land said that they had been guided by the top of *Ark*'s mast, which was sticking out above the fog like a signpost. 'There she is, God bless her!' they thought, and groped their way in through the intervening murk, until in a quick flurry of thinning mist they glimpsed the curve of the roundown and rushed for the lights of home before the cruel fog could swallow them again.

Aboard ship they counted. Eight Skuas came back out of the fog. After that there was silence around the ship. The others never came back.

The survivors, who did not feel very much like talking, sketched in the outlines of what they had done and seen at Trondheim.

The Germans had had everything ready for them, 109's, 110's and a forest of ack-ack guns. Coast watchers gave the alarm as soon as the Skuas crossed the coast.

Then they still had fifty miles to fly before they came to Trondheim, so the Germans there had about twenty minutes in which to prepare a warm welcome.

As the Skuas approached Trondheim at 11,500 feet the Messerschmitts fell upon them. Flak from ship and shore burst all around their aircraft and broke up the formation, so that each machine attacked alone.

They had seen their target. The *Scharnhorst* was down there.

They dived straight into the battlecruiser's red-hot barrage, the German fighters all the time fastening on them like hounds.

It was worse than any of them could have imagined. There was little time to see where their bombs went. Those who got away did so by keeping low and threading their way out under cover of the mist. The only hits anyone claimed were two vivid flashes abaft *Scharnhorst*'s funnel. In fact it was discovered that only one hit had been made, the bomb failing to explode.

The *Ark* had lost nearly half the Skua crews who had taken off. When the survivors had returned and the losses were known, a man from one of the guns' crews came up to Everett and said quietly,

'We want you to know, sir, that we're all very sorry about Mr Finch-Noyes.'

Ned, great comedian, great character, was gone. *Ark Royal*, and especially Ark Royal Productions, would never be quite the same without him.

Petty Officer Cunningham, who had been in *Ark*'s first victory against the Dorniers, was made prisoner after the raid. The Germans interrogated him.

'You came from the *Ark Royal*, didn't you?' they asked him.

'Don't be bloody silly!' said Cunningham. 'You sank the *Ark Royal* last year. Don't you remember?'

The Germans looked embarrassed. Eventually, however, the need for truth got the better of propaganda. Francke, they admitted, was not the hero he had been made out to be. He had taken off as one of a formation of bombers sent to attack a force of British ships in the North Sea. In fact the force which he and his fellow pilots were meant to bomb was the southern force of cruisers. But Francke lost the rest of his formation. Flying on alone through the cloudy weather he suddenly burst out over a group of British ships.

It was not the target he had been briefed to attack, but he saw a carrier and decided to drop his bomb on her. When he returned from his lone attack he could not be certain whether he had hit the carrier or not. A reconnaissance was therefore sent out to find the force he had bombed.

This time, however, they located the cruiser force which Francke had been supposed to bomb in the first place. Naturally they saw no carrier. Their information plus Francke's report of a hit or a very near miss was all Goebbels needed to announce to the world that the Luftwaffe had blitzed the British Fleet and sunk its pride and joy, the *Ark Royal*.

It was a sad voyage home across the North Sea for the *Ark* after Trondheim. Everybody felt they had had enough for a while. So there was relief when the captain announced that they were going back to the Clyde. The ship, overdue for a refit, would go into drydock at Greenock and the men would go on leave.

CHAPTER VI

BIRDS OF A FEATHER

WHEN spring came in 1940 and the great mine which the Germans had been preparing all through the winter of the 'phoney war' blew up in our faces, setting off in its train the half-expected Fascist attack in the Mediterranean, one thing became clear. Air power would win the war. Thereafter, whoever was superior in the air dominated the other.

Norway was won by air power. The Germans had more of it, and in the beginning used it more imaginatively. What small resistance we did put up in the air was only made possible by the use of carriers. The Germans swiftly occupied all the good aerodromes in Norway, and the country itself was out of effective range of aircraft flying from airfields in England. When there were no airfields ashore for us, the carriers, steaming off the coast, provided all the air support. When we cleared Skaanland and Bardufoss, carriers brought the Gladiators and Hurricanes across from England which fought so successfully there. If we had had enough carriers we might have held Norway.

When the *Ark Royal* steamed sadly into Scapa Flow after the attack on *Scharnhorst* in Trondheim, lack of air power was already helping the Germans to win the campaign in France. Our few squadrons there were being decimated, and we were already drawing in our horns, keeping an essential nucleus of fighter squadrons at home. The Fleet Air Arm was low in strength too, seriously cut down by the fighting in Norway and the loss of the *Courageous* and *Glorious*.

With France almost beaten Italy declared war upon us. On 11th June bombers of the powerful Regia Aeronautica attacked Malta, where the fighter defence consisted of four obsolescent Sea Gladiator fighters flown most gallantly and skilfully by volunteer pilots of the Royal Air Force. Fascist bombers and fighters in large numbers now threatened us from both sides of the Mediterranean.

In fact hostile air power made loud the skies all around us. We for our part had only a handful of planes with which to defend our homeland, our lifeline of ships at sea in the Atlantic and Mediterranean, and our already sorely tried fleet, which had already lost heavily in destroyers and carriers.

Our aeroplanes were very few, both on land and at sea. It was our pride, however, that the men who flew them were the best in the world. In that belief lay our only hope.

The Royal Navy knew only too well, after Norway was Dunkirk, just what lack of fighter cover could mean to a warship. Under that ceiling of Stukas and Savoias they would be lucky to survive.

With this in mind the Navy could not afford to take any additional chances with the threat from the enemy's powerful aggregate of battleships, battlecruisers and big cruisers. The Italians had a large, fast, modern fleet, the Germans the nucleus of a very able and dangerous one. In ports all along the North Sea and Atlantic coasts German pocket battleships, battlecruisers, and the immensely strong new battleships *Bismarck* and *Tirpitz*, would be able to break out and savage our convoys. Some were at sea already. The Italian Battle Fleet lay in Taranto harbour, ready to put to sea, a 'fleet in being' potent and menacing.

And this was not all. If France surrendered, who would have the benefit of the French Fleet?

When France finally capitulated on 22nd June the problem became acute. At Oran, in Algeria, and at Mersel-Kebir, close by, was a powerful French fleet under Admiral Gensoul. With him he had the two new battle-cruisers *Dunkerque* and *Strasbourg*, two older battleships, and several light cruisers and destroyers. Here was another 'fleet in being', strong enough to alter the balance of power in the Mediterranean.

The situation was embarrassing and difficult. Delay was dangerous. Gensoul must not be allowed to slip out with his fleet and join our enemies. He must be made to see reason, either by diplomatic persuasion, or, if that failed, by force.

It was as a result of this urgent situation that *Ark Royal* did not get her leave after all, but made instead for Gibraltar at full speed after only three days in Scapa. Another carrier was in any case badly needed in the Mediterranean to protect the fleet and help it to hold the Italians in check, and the Oran crisis precipitated her arrival. In more ways than one *Ark Royal* was the very ship for this particularly delicate job.

The tide of war was running faster and ever faster. Air power, in German hands, called the tune that made it flow. The ships of the Royal Navy, and especially her carriers, were flung in now to try to slow it down before it could surround and finally engulf us.

Gibraltar had forgotten what the *Ark* looked like. They had not seen her since peacetime days, when she had called there during her training cruise. She looked huge and strange lying there at the wharf, especially to the new men who came out from Britain to join her there.

Kenneth Lord, a newly joined naval writer, thought she looked bigger than ever, towering there seventy feet out of the water. The first time he had seen her was in Portsmouth when he was at the torpedo school at *Vernon*. He had looked out one morning and there she was, dwarfing the big semaphore tower in the dockyard. What a wonderful ship she was! How thrilled he felt to see her at such close quarters and to step aboard her as one of her ship's company!

On board everyone seemd to be going mad. All was frantic, feverish haste: officers and men rushing hither and thither at the double; lift bells clanging; a deafening clangour from the hangar workshops; the stink of air-craft fuel dominating the close, stifling atmosphere that pervaded the endless warren of passages. How would he ever get used to it all? How could he possibly do a job of work here?

He was given no time to feel his way, but was flung straight into the whirlpool of bustle to sink or swim. It was the way of the *Ark*. 'Purpose knows no rest' had become a terse 'flat out' in the blunt language of the lower-deck. Kenneth was expected as a matter of course to pitch straight in and work flat out in the captain's office.

Ark Royal's new captain worked harder than anyone, and spent much of his time in consultation with Vice-Admiral Somerville, the Flag Officer of Force H at Gibraltar. Power had gone and Captain C. S. Holland had replaced him. He was a very different kind of naval officer to their old captain, and the old hands were still weighing him up.

Where Power had been bluff, unyielding and forth-right, Holland was elegant, mannered, and friendly. Power had led by sheer character, Holland ruled by diplomacy. Sid Tanner, who, as captain's joiner, came much into contact with him, as he had with Power, could not help comparing them. Holland was tall and fair, and had the appearances of a dandy in contrast to Power. It took a long time for rough matelots to realise that aftershave lotion does not make a man soft or in any way less of a fine leader.

Sid sniffed a bit, often literally, at the captain's elegant ways, and came to the conclusion that he had picked them up in France. It was certainly true that Captain Holland, as Naval Attaché at the British Embassy in Paris immediately before the war, and later as British Naval Liaison Officer with Admiral Darlan, had acquired a love of France and a host of French friends.

One of the closest of these was Admiral Gensoul. The French admiral, who now lay with his fleet at Oran, silent and sullen, had only a few months previously given a dinner party in Holland's honour. Now the two friends were to meet in very different circumstances, circumstances which Captain Holland could only feel as intolerable.

Force H, with some additional ships, was destined for Oran. At Gibraltar had been collected a strong striking force. Admiral Somerville flew his flag in *Hood*, and with her were *Valiant, Resolution, Ark Royal*, two cruisers, and eleven destroyers.

Ark Royal had a special part to play. Her aircraft were to be carried, of course, to spot for the fleet, should it be necessary to use force against the French vessels. But it was hoped that in Captain Holland she would bring a more desirable weapon to bear upon Admiral Gensoul – the reminder of a long-standing alliance made warmer by personal friendship. Holland was to go ashore at Oran and attempt to negotiate with Gensoul in an effort to strike a reasonable bargain without recourse to violence. If he failed, and his former friend and colleague spurned the velvet glove . . . Captain Holland, and there were many like him in the British ships, did not care to dwell upon the possible consequences.

It was only a short run across the coast of Algeria.

Force H lay in Gibraltar harbour waiting, while a stream of signals flowed between Somerville's flagship and the Admiralty.

At 2.25 a.m. on 1st July the Admiralty signalled to Admiral Somerville:

'Be prepared for Catapult 3rd July.'

Diplomacy, then, had two days in which to triumph. 'Catapult' was the name for the assault by force. Early the same afternoon Somerville replied:

'After talk with Holland and others Vice-Admiral Force H is impressed with their view that the use of force should be avoided at all costs. Holland considers offensive action on our part would alienate all French wherever they are.'

The reply came at 6.20:

'Firm intention of H.M. Government that if French will not accept any of your alternatives they must be destroyed.'

That evening Mr Churchill requested the Admiralty to send the following message to Admiral Somerville:

'You are charged with one of the most disagreeable and difficult tasks that a British Admiral has ever been faced with, but we have complete confidence in you and rely on you to carry it out relentlessly.'

At first light on 3rd July Force H sailed from Gibraltar and arrived off Oran. Captain Holland had been sent ahead in a destroyer, and reached Oran at 8 a.m.

The French authorities would not permit the destroyer to pass the boom, but allowed Captain Holland to proceed into the harbour by motor-launch. Admiral Gensoul, however, refused to see him. Holland had the British proposals passed to him.

The main alternatives offered to the French admiral were either to co-operate with the British Fleet, or to sail under British supervision to a British port. The crews of the ships would then be sent home to France and the ships themselves impounded, to be handed back to the French Navy after the war. Failing the acceptance of either of these proposals, the admiral was required to take his ships to the French West Indies, or to scuttle them within six hours.

If he rejected all these terms the British Government would agree to the demilitarisation of the ships in their present berths, as long as such measures were effectively carried out.

If he did not do this, Admiral Somerville had orders to use 'whatever force might be necessary' to prevent the French ships from falling into the hands of our enemies.

Admiral Gensoul studied these conditions, then received Captain Holland. For hour after hour the two men discussed them, point by point. Holland exercised all the persuasion in his power to prevail upon Gensoul, but in the end the French Admiral refused to comply with any of the alternatives, and Captain Holland left the *Dunkerque* to return to Force H and prepare his own ship for the most unpleasant action he would ever be likely to face.

When, at 6.26 p.m., the Admiralty signalled, 'French ships must comply with our terms or sink themselves or be sunk by you before dark,' the big guns of Force H had already opened fire. At six o'clock Somerville reported himself heavily engaged. The heavy shells of *Hood*, *Valiant*, and *Resolution* fell with shattering force upon the French ships. The officers directing this fire did so with bitter feelings. Bob Everett, above the battle in a Swordfish, watched the destruction with a heavy heart, for he had been born and brought up in France. 'At the Admiralty also,' wrote Mr Churchill, 'there was manifest emotion.'

The Swordfish from *Ark Royal* directed the fire of the fleet, and five others, led by Everett, went down to water level and dropped mines across the entrance to Mers-el-Kebir harbour.

So far the battleship *Bretagne* had been sunk and the flagship *Dunkerque* damaged and forced to run aground;

the battleship *Provence* and some smaller ships were seriously damaged. It was not a good score for twenty-four fifteen-inch guns.

Strasbourg had got away altogether, stealing out of the harbour under cover of darkness, with an escort of five destroyers. She fled east at full speed, with Swordfish from the *Ark* after her.

It was the first time ship-borne torpedo-bombers had attacked a battleship a sea, and the torpedo pilots hoped for great things. They found the battlecruiser fleeing at twenty-eight knots under heavy smoke with a destroyer screen around her. With no previous battle experience of this kind to guide them the pilots dropped their torpedoes too far away from their target and *Strasbourg* disappeared in the darkness.

Dunkerque was not yet completely immobilised. Next day, in the darkness of early morning, a wave of Swordfish took off and flew down the first rays of the sun that glinted off the battlecruiser's flanks as she lay aground. Four of their six torpedoes hit the target.

Much as the Fleet Air Arm pilots deplored 'this melancholy action', as Mr Churchill called it, they could not help but feel a certain elation at the ease with which they had done their work. In bad light at dusk half a dozen little aeroplanes had overhauled a fast battlecruiser at speed and attacked her, when the orthodox capital ships of Force H had been powerless. Under cover of darkness they had also surprised a capital ship in harbour and had put her out of action when the concentrated gunfire of three great ships had failed to do so. With more experience, they felt, they could do very much better. Perhaps the Italian Fleet would give them the chance.

Three days later they were fighting the Italians. Admiral Cunningham, with the Mediterranean Fleet based on Alexandria, and Admiral Somerville, with Force H, turned now, with the French threat removed, to the job of keeping the 'Italian Lake' clear of Italians, so that General Wavell in North Africa could be supplied and his army built up to face the imminent attack by the Italian Army in Libya. This entailed the protection of convoys supplying the British Army as well as attacks upon Italian ports and airfields to keep the enemy bottled up in his home waters.

An Italian Cant seaplane shadowing a British force on the afternoon of 9th July had only just managed to radio the news that the *Ark Royal* was present when three of her Skuas appeared on his tail and shot him down. His message, however, brought forty S.M.79 bombers over the carrier. They dropped a hundred bombs, but the Skuas made them miss and shot down four of them, badly damaging several others. The odds were very heavy, but the pilots of the *Ark*, like those of any of the Navy's overworked carriers, were already used to that. They would be glad, nevertheless, when the new ships of the *Illustrious* class, with their armoured flight-decks, put to sea to give them a helping hand. Meanwhile they carried on cheerfully alone.

Soon the *Ark* became an accepted part of the Gibraltar scene, and every merchant ship which came within her orbit came to know her and bless her. Wherever the *Ark Royal* was her famous 'luck' seemed to go with her, and some of it brushed off on everyone else.

Her old hands began to get acquainted with 'The Rock' once more, and those green hands like Kenneth Lord who had 'just joined' began to discover The Universal, where the beer flowed freely to the music of the all-girls' band, the Imperial, where Kenneth used to go for hot coffee and some of their special tiny cakes after a brisk swim and a laze in the sun at Catalan Bay, and the R.N. cinema, where you sat and stewed in your own perspiration and cursed the intervals and break-downs when they always played 'The Flight of the Bumble Bee'.

As usual *Ark Royal* herself supplied plenty of first-class entertainment. She was especially keen on sport, and her football team were her best ambassadors ashore, and among her chummy ships of Force H. For a long while they remained unbeatable. Most of the team had played together in the *Courageous* and in the *Ark* herself for a long time, and were usually a match for the army teams on the Rock, many of whose players were professionals from well-known British clubs called up for the army. A match between the *Ark Royal* team and the army was always the signal for a gala day. The matelots were always well entertained by the army, who perhaps suffered from pangs of conscience after their unhampered pillaging of the beer boat when Force H was out on an operation.

Water polo was another strong favourite in the ship. Percy Hancock was in the *Ark*'s team, and he always had a quiet laugh at the sergeant of Marines, a pillar of the side, whenever the great man stripped for action and plunged in. In his full dress uniform he was a fine, smart figure of a soldier, complete in every meticulous detail, with an exquisitely cultivated, superbly waxed moustache to add the final touch to the whole splendid picture of martial power and pomp. As the team took to the water he would stand poised on the ship's side in his bathing costume for a moment, twiddle his gorgeous moustaches, then dive in. His face as he came up for the first time was a study in contrasts – those wonderful handlebars, his pride and joy, hanging all wet and limp, and the sergeant himself looking like Alice's walrus! 'I know now why sergeant-major's cultivate 'em!' thought Percy.

Captain Holland gave all sports his whole-hearted encouragement. In the evenings at sea, between the periodic flying off of patrols, he made it standard practice to get out the mats and the vaulting horse and set them up on the flight-deck in the lee of the island. The P.T.I. then led volunteers in physical training and 'follow my leader' vaulting exercises. Almost invariably the captain himself would come down from the bridge to join in.

This happy spirit made everyone fight the better. It

made the men who worked the ship herself feel that they were defending something real, a part of the feeling fighter pilots had at home when they saw the Luftwaffe over London.

It made the natural élan of her airmen sparkle with greater vivacity. In his cabin, in a swinging cage, Bob Everett kept a canary, and many another pilot had one. They didn't exactly carry them up into action perched on their shoulders like a pirate's parrot, but whenever the planes were up and fighting over the fleet and the eagles of the Regia Aeronautica were squawking and losing their feathers, the little birds of the *Ark* never sang so sweetly. . . . They, and the outnumbered Skuas and Swordfish, and all the hard-pressed fighters of the Few fighting desperately now at home, were birds of a feather, it seemed, for when the massed Axis birds of prey appeared, they all gave voice together.

The sailors sang a lot, too, mostly nostalgic popular tunes that took them home. The favourites were 'Room 504' and 'All the things you are', and they sang songs from the shows which the ship herself put on in the hangar.

At other times the hangar became a cinema. The *Ark Royal* loved to go to the pictures, and in between periods of action in the Mediterranean, they were given the chance to help make a picture themselves.

Someone had the excellent idea of making a film with a Fleet Air Arm background. Carrier-flying, of course, lent itself particularly well to filming, even in those days before colour and CinemaScope, and when Roy Kellino and his camera team came out from England to film some of the picture on board *Ark Royal*, the ship that was always in the news and a 'natural' for film making, everybody gave him enthusiastic support. Bob Everett, with his almost professional interest in filming, fitted out a Swordfish especially to carry Kellino and his film camera, and flew him many miles around the Mediterranean while he shot the ship and her aircraft from all angles. Alas, a good film was ruined in the studio. The shots taken of *Ark Royal* were mixed with a story of unbelievable corn and hokum. All that splendid footage of film was wasted, along with the talents of John Clements, Michael Rennie, and Michael Wilding, who played three intrepid airmen competing for the affections of the Admiral's daughter, not to mention Ann Todd and Jane Baxter. All of these fine players survived the ghastly mediocrity of the film, but it could only make them wince today to remember that they once appeared in a film called 'Ships With Wings'.

So dire did the Admiralty consider 'Ships With Wings' that, in conjunction with the shooting of a Fleet Air Arm instructional film, they had made an antidote to it called 'Find, Fix, and Strike', in which Compton Bennett, Anthony Kimmins and Bob Everett all had a hand. Everett had left *Ark Royal* by then, and had his own squadron in *Illustrious* when some of the closing shots of the film were made aboard her. Everett, who had worked at Ealing on the earlier part of the film featured in this part of it as the 'batsman'.

'Ships With Wings' was a flop, and *Ark Royal* soon put on a much better flying show herself at Cagliari on the southern coast of Sardinia.

Before the raid, which was *Ark Royal*'s first attack on the Italian homeland, Admiral Somerville signalled to the carrier:

'The object of this operation is to test the quality of the ice-cream.'

Everett featured in this show too, leading a section of mine-laying Swordfish. It was a difficult operation, conducted in pitch darkness with the aircraft flying in the face of sixty-knot headwinds. An attack planned for dawn was finally made in full daylight, as the main force of dive-bombers at first mistook their objective and had to retrace their steps. The mine-layers were laying their eggs neatly across the harbour from a height of fifty feet when the dive-bombers arrived and were being engaged by the coastal batteries, one of which was firing six-inch shells in the hope that the aircraft would be wrecked by the geysers of spray which they threw up.

The dive-bombers attacked the aerodrome and sea-planes in the harbour, screaming down through the fiercest anti-aircraft fire. Only one enemy fighter attacked the force, and he was much more of a help than a hindrance as the batteries below ceased fire while he was engaging our aircraft. He made a furious attack on one of the Swordfish until all his ammunition was gone, then came up and flew close alongside so that its guns could not bear. The midshipman in the rear cockpit of the Swordfish immediately flourished a revolver and took him on with that. Shaken, the Italian banked away and was not seen again.

Operation Smash, as this was called, was a definite success. Hangars, buildings and aircraft were wrecked for the loss of one Swordfish, the crew of which were taken prisoner after force-landing on the airfield which they had just bombed. The rest were scattered and flew the hundred and fifty miles back to the ship independently, covered by the *Ark*'s Skuas. The last Swordfish to reach the ship landed-on with less than five gallons of petrol left in the tank, having been in the air for four and a half hours.

On 2nd and 3rd September they went back again and did Operation Grab. There was more to it this time than merely 'testing the quality of the ice-cream'. The Government had decided to send reinforcements to the Mediterranean in the shape of three armoured regiments for General Wavell, who faced an immensely powerful Italian army in Libya, and the new carrier *Illustrious*, together with the battleship *Valiant* and two anti-aircraft cruisers, for Admiral Cunningham. The naval reinforcements were to go through the Mediterranean, but this route was considered too dangerous for the army transports, which were sent to Suez via the Cape.

The reinforcements sailed at the end of August. Force

H escorted the naval contingent as far as Sicily, and the Mediterranean Fleet took them over from there. At the same time Admiral Cunningham brought a convoy through from Alexandria to Malta, and *Valiant* and the new cruisers landed guns and ammunition at Malta.

Ark Royal's part in the operation was to create a diversion by bombing Cagliari to keep the bombers there away from the convoy. They made two attacks in bad visibility and dropped their bombs by the light of parachute flares. The whole force reached the Sicilian channel unmolested, and Operation Grab was a complete success.

When the *Ark*'s planes were at Cagliari one of the ship's numerous cats gave birth to twins which were immediately named Smash and Grab, the Cagliari Twins.

Force H had tested the ice-cream and found the quality mixed but mostly indifferent. The pilots of *Ark Royal* felt they could just about cope with the Italians, who seemed to lack an real zeal for their cause, although individual pilots frequently showed great daring and bravery in their attacks on our ships, especially the torpedo-bomber pilots. In our hands air power was helping to stem the tide of the Axis blitz. *Ark Royal*, ever first in achievement, was plugging the dyke against the flood of Italian arms, so full at first, but now becoming sluggish. However, it was still spurting through in a thousand places.

Jack Bishop's job, which entailed repairing the guns as well as fighting them, was a formidable one. At sea he and the other ordnance men took their action stations at the various guns, standing by to repair any breakdown and keep the guns firing. As soon as they returned to harbour their work really started, inspecting the guns and making them ready again.

When the ship was under attack it was always worst for those below decks, especially the ones who had never been in action before, like Kenneth Lord. Although he was a writer, there was nothing to do in the captain's office when *Ark Royal* was at sea taking her merchant-men through Mare Nostrum, and he was stationed deep down below in one of the main magazines. Many a time he thought they were forgotten men down there. Being a day man he was not subject to watch routines, and once he spent over thirty hours in the magazine without a break.

They reached the magazine by way of a series of armoured hatches, each of which had to be clipped down behind them. The last hatch was under the supervision of an old stoker, who used to shut them in with great relish. It was his duty to sit all alone by a huge stopcock, with which he could flood the magazine in a matter of seconds, in an emergency. Down in the magazine they were really in the bowels of the ship, surrounded by high-explosive shells, which they had to feed continuously without let-up to the guns above. All the time the metal bulkheads around them and the warm deck-plates under their feet vibrated and trembled. A near miss from a bomb, a piece of shrapnel hitting the ship's side, echoed through the padlocked spaces and made the heart leap sickeningly. Above them was one battened-down hatch-way, watched over by a solitary man.

But there were lulls now and again, and these were always the signal for some of Chef Vatcher's famous 'tiddie oggies'. These juicy pasties were the chief cook's specialities, and he must have made thousands of them.

As this long summer of 1940 wore on the thoughts of all aboard the *Ark* turned more and more to home. As they fought off the Italians they worried about their families at home whom the fighters of the R.A.F. were now struggling desperately to protect. They longed for a look at home again, even if there was nothing much to do there except sit in an air-raid shelter. The ship too was in need of a visit to a drydock. Now, with the Italian effort in the Mediterranean beginning to flag, and the *Illustrious* with the Mediterranean Fleet, seemed to be the time to send her home. The Italian Fleet skulked in harbour and did not seem inclined to venture out. The *Ark*'s torpedo bombers would have loved the chance to get in amongst those fat battleships in Taranto, but before she could tackle anything like that she needed a refit and replacements for her squadrons.

Before she could be released, however, another emergency arose out of the French situation. The British Government was seriously worried that the Vichy French might gain control of the French West African port of Dakar, which had been so useful to us in the protection of our convoys round the Cape, but which under German control could be just as big a menace to them. The situation became urgent and, in spite of inside knowledge of the likelihood of heavy opposition, the main body of an Anglo-Free French expedition sailed for West Africa from home ports on 31st August. The escorting force was under Admiral J. H. D. Cunningham, and would be joined later by units of Force H from Gibraltar.

But, before the two forces had joined, Cunningham, still three hundred miles north-west of Dakar, heard on 11th September that a force of three Vichy cruisers and three big destroyers had come through the Straits of Gibraltar and were heading south. By this time *Ark Royal*, with *Barham* and four destroyers from the Home Fleet had left Gibraltar to join Admiral Cunningham. Admiral Somerville was still at Gibraltar with *Renown* and some destroyers.

But Somerville had received no orders, either direct from the Admiralty or from Admiral North, Flag Officer Commanding the North Atlantic Station, to intercept the French ships. Admiral North, also at Gibraltar, was in no position to give him such an order. Firstly, although Somerville was his junior, he had become accustomed to thinking of Force H as a 'detached force' which took its orders direct from the Admiralty. Secondly, he had interpreted a misleading and ambiguous series of Admiralty directives to read that Vichy warships must not be interfered with provided they were not making for an enemy-controlled port. When he saw that this particular force was making for Dakar he saw, therefore, no cause for action. The business of our own expedition at the same port might have made him change his mind – if he had known of that business. But the orders for Operation Menace, as it was called, had not been issued to him.

So the Vichy ships, heading for Dakar to help prevent the very thing which our force had sailed to achieve, got through. At mid-day on 11th September the Admiralty realised the object of their sortie and ordered Somerville to raise steam for full speed. At 4.30 p.m. he sailed with orders to prevent the French ships from entering Dakar but not to bar them from Casablanca. By the time he was at sea, however, the French ships had reached Casablanca. He at once established a patrol line between them and Dakar, to the south.

At 3.30 on 13th September aircraft reported to Admiral Cunningham, now at Freetown with most of his escorting Force M together, that the French ships had left Casablanca heading for Dakar. Shortly after they had left, Somerville's blockading force had headed for Gibraltar to refuel and so missed them. Cunningham gathered all the ships he could and started to patrol off Dakar on the evening of the 14th, but he had scarcely begun when he heard from the Vichy radio that their ships were now in Dakar. *Ark Royal*'s Swordfish confirmed it next morning. By now the troopships of our expedition had reached Freetown and Cunningham returned there.

By this time the Admiralty had lost all confidence in the venture, but Cunningham and General de Gaulle thought it could still be accomplished, and by 21st September the whole force had sailed from Freetown for Dakar. On board the *Ark Royal* were twenty Free Frenchmen and three French Luciole planes. As she approached Dakar on the 23rd the carrier flew off two of the Lucioles and three Swordfish to land Gaullist representatives who were hoping to pave the way for a bloodless occupation by the Allied troops.

The aircraft were allowed to land without any trouble, but the Swordfish pilots were uneasy and kept a watchful eye open and their guns at the ready while their passengers disembarked. Then they wasted no time in taking and returning to the ship.

They were lucky to escape. Their passengers were shot and other emissaries fired on, and by eleven o'clock our ships were under fire from the Vichy ships, which included the battlecruiser *Richelieu*, and the shore batteries. *Cumberland* and two destroyers were hit.

At 11.45 a.m. the Allied Force broadcast an ultimatum to the Vichy Governor-General, demanding that he accept their terms by 6 a.m. the next morning and allow their troops to occupy Dakar to prevent the Germans from using it. He answered, 'We confirm that we will oppose all landings.'

An attempted landing to the east of the port was repulsed with heavy loss of life. Then, in the thickening fog, communications between the various sections of our force broke down. At dawn our big ships prepared to bombard the Vichy warships and shore batteries. Planes from *Ark Royal* took off to bomb the *Richelieu* and the other heavy ships. Fire from the French ships and shore batteries combined with an effective smoke screen and the ever-thickening fog forced our ships to withdraw. When *Barham* and *Resolution* tried to renew the action in the afternoon they got the worst of it and *Resolution* was hit four times. *Ark Royal*'s aircraft could do no better.

On 25th September our whole force tried again, but at 9 a.m. the *Resolution* was badly damaged by a torpedo and by mid-day the situation had become hopeless. In the afternoon came the Admiralty order cancelling Operation Menace. From the start it had been abortive and had only resulted in useless bloodshed, bad relations, and serious damage to several of our priceless warships. The Navy cut its losses and hurriedly sent the warships engaged back to the various points where their presence was so urgently needed.

Ark Royal withdrew from the blue and gold battle-field where she had campaigned all summer and sailed for Liverpool.

While she had been away showing the Italians how effective even a handful of aircraft could be, the Royal Air Force had been showing the same thing to the world in the skies over Britain. Fleet Air Arm pilots had fought in R.A.F. squadrons throughout that glorious summer and had helped to beat the Luftwaffe, who had now switched all their attacks to the hours of darkness, when they came over and blitzed our ports and cities.

Ark Royal ran into the air-aids as soon as she berthed in the Gladstone Dock. Her ship's company went on seven days' leave, and many of them were bombed at home as well. Some of them never came back to *Ark Royal*, but joined other ships. New men were drafted up to Liverpool to take their places.

B: his time the first batches of naval ratings to be trained as air mechanics had begun to find their way into Fleet Air Arm squadrons, replacing by degrees the Royal Air Force men who had stayed on to see the new branch off to a good start. On 1st July, when *Ark Royal* was at Oran, a number of the new naval air mechanics arrived at R.N.A.S., Worthy Down, to join a new unit, No. 808 Fleet Fighter Squadron, which was forming up with the new Fairey Fulmar fighters, eight-gun, all metal, two-seater machines designed specially for carrier work.

They started to work up as a squadron at Worthy Down, but made a hurried departure for St Merryn in Cornwall after a bomb had hit the hangar they were using. From St Merryn they were shunted practically all the way from Land's End to John o' Groats to an R.A.F. aerodrome at Castletown, near Thurso, in Scotland. They arrived there after a journey of forty-two hours and began a strenuous routine of working up.

120

They were split up into three watches: one duty, one stand-by, and one off-duty. The duty watch would turn-to at some unearthly hour of the morning to service the aircraft ready for a dawn patrol of three Fulmars, with three more standing by at immediate readiness. As the planes returned from patrol they were serviced by the duty watch until relieved by the stand-by watch who meanwhile had been eating breakfast in an old barn, which was all the dining space they had. This routine went on all day, with the machines being filled up as fast as they landed. The duty watch slept in the office building, fully dressed and ready to run out to the three Fulmars in position at the end of the runway. The watch off duty used to go to the Masonic hall in the village three miles from the field, where they were able to wash for the first time in three days, and do their dhobeying. Water had to be carried from a stream; they used to bathe there until some old ladies complained. Meals were taken in the local school, a mile away. The evenings were spent in the local pub, if you were lucky. The local was very small, and half a dozen thirsty air mechanics just about filled it. The rest had to be content with tea and buns at the Church of Scotland hut.

The weeks went by, and gradually a buzz began to grow that the squadron was off shortly to sea. It wasn't difficult to fill in the gap. There was only one ship it could be – we didn't have that many! It must be the *Ark Royal*. Good-oh!

They went on to Donibristle for ten days, then made for Liverpool on 19th October. It was dark and raining when they got to Gladstone Dock, and there was an air raid on. They groped their way aboard their first ship not knowing whether they were on the port or the starboard side, or which was for'ard and which was aft, and they soon lost themselves. But they were all immensely thrilled. So were the new telegraphist air-gunners of the squadron, some of whom joined about the same time.

When war was declared in September 1939 a young

apprentice named O'Nion at the Austin Motor Company at Longbridge, in Birmingham, began to notice advertisements in the papers about joining the Navy and flying on aircraft carriers. It seemed a life full of excitement, foreign travel, and good prospects all round. Without telling his father he went to the recruiting office in Birmingham and passed the examination for naval aircrew. He didn't much like the idea of signing on for twelve years, but there was no other alternative at the time. He signed.

The worst part of it all was telling his father. Mr O'Nion had been for thirty years a manager with Austins, and wanted his son to follow in his footsteps. It took three days to convince him that his son did not want that kind of life. By that time he had received his travelling orders to report to Portsmouth Barracks.

He did his flying training at Eastleigh, and finally qualified in August 1940, right in the middle of the Battle of Britain. He and those other new T.A.G.s were told that they were to join the famous *Ark Royal* at Liverpool, and be ready to join up with No. 808 Fleet Fighter Squadron, then at Donibristle.

They joined *Ark Royal* late at night. She was still in Gladstone Dock in the middle of her refit. Half the ship's company was on leave, and the ship was in a state of chaos. It was hard, for a while, finding their way around in darkness on a huge ship honeycombed with passages, especially for landlubbers who had never been on a ship in their lives before. Eventually they found a space to sling their hammocks amongst all the wires, pipes, and paraphernalia left scattered about. Next morning they found to their surprise that in the blackout they had slung them over the dockyard workers who were asleep on the deck below.

Next morning, while they were doing their joining routine, they had their first real glimpse of the ship. She was not an impressive sight. There were workmen everywhere, and foremen shouting orders, and the decks were littered with gear. The flight-deck and hangar-decks were strewn with a higgledy-piggledy miscellany of stores: drums of cable; pots of paint; gas cylinders; drums of oil; and packing-cases full of aeroplane parts. O'Nion wondered if the workmen knew where it all had to go, but after a few days things seemed to sort themselves out, and the ship began to take on a clean and tidy appearance. They could now walk round the passageways without fear of tripping over a pipe, a power cable, or a dockyard matey. The squadron messes were on the port side, running down the side of the hangar-decks – a convenient arrangement as it gave them quick access to the hangars or flight-deck.

By now, 'hostilities only' conscripts were beginning to come to the ship. One of these was young wireman Claydon, an electrician in civilian life, who had only recently passed his trade test at St Vincent, and had come to *Ark Royal* now to do a naval version of the same job. Four of the newly made wiremen who had become pals on the course arrived in Pompey late one afternoon in October, and after being victualled-in were told to report to the Master-at-Arms' office to do joining routine. They arrived there full of hope for end-of-course leave. All they got was a leer from the man behind the little window who said,

'Ah, yes, four wiremen. You know where you're going, don't you? The *Ark Royal*!'

They way he said it sounded like a threat.

About three hundred men were on the draft next morning to Liverpool. Half of them were for *Ark Royal*, half for the *Hood*. Claydon could not know what a lucky escape he had had.

Old *Ark Royal* men came back from leave to mingle with the new ones. It was not a long refit, she was too badly needed for sea for that – only seven days' leave for each watch. The day before leave had started from the ship Euston Station had been badly bombed, and the liberty men eventually went south on a special train

123

which by-passed London. Before they left Lime Street a bunch of them went to a pub and took away a stock of beer for the long journey. That ride took them twelve hours, and all the bottles finished up on the line. The ship, however, suffered very little damage that night. One man was hurt, being slightly cut about the face, but he could get no sympathy. Everybody said he must have had a drop too much the night before and fallen in the dock.

After a few days of this *Ark* left the drydock and put to sea, having embarked more flying and maintenance personnel. As they pulled slowly away from the dockside young Claydon found himself standing at one end of the great ship – he later found out it was the bows – feeling utterly strange and bewildered. Seeing a few people on the roof of a building he waved to them half-heartedly, feeling very small and insignificant, and wondering what he had let himself in for.

First port of call was the Clyde. They were fog-bound there for one day, then put out into the Irish Sea to embark aircraft.

C.O. of the new Fulmar squadron was Lieutenant-Commander R. C. Tillard, and the senior observer Lieutenant Somerville, a nephew of the flag officer, Force H. They and the aircrew had been with the squadron all along were to fly the aircraft aboard, with a few ground-crew in the back seats as passengers.

As *Ark Royal* turned into the wind O'Nion and the other air-gunners and observers watched their new squadron eagerly from the catwalk. Most of them, being aircrew, were superstitious, and were a bit uneasy when they counted thirteen Fulmars in the circuit.

The first twelve landed safely aboard. Then the thirteenth came in. Just as he was about to touch down the pilot seemed to change his mind. Trying to get airborne again, his port wing dipped, hit the edge of the flight-deck, and spun the Fulmar over into the sea.

The aircraft was lost, but the pilot, Midshipman Guy,

and his passenger, Naval Airman Yates, got off with a ducking and a bad shaking up. They were picked up by the destroyer crash-boat and returned to the ship.

Later that day the ship's company was told that the *Ark* was bound for Gibraltar and Force H again. On their way they escorted the liner *Pasteur*, packed with troops for North Africa. The voyage was uneventful, except for the landlubbers, many of whom were seasick on this their first voyage. O'Nion counted himself lucky in being immune from seasickness. The truth was that he had been so horribly sick in the air when he started flying that there was just nothing left to be seasick with. Others, less lucky, found a quiet spot near the ship's side and communed with nature for the next few days.

They tied up safely in Gibraltar harbour inside the Mole alongside Flagstaff Steps, and joined once more the happy ranks of the Force H Club. As usual the beer ship was not there when they arrived.

'She'll come in just as we leave, you see!' the old hands said.

Ark did the next 'club run', as Admiral Somerville called them, early in November. They had come out just in time to take part in a great combined action which was to involve all the ships of the Mediterranean Fleet, with manifold objectives.

Only the senior officers knew the whole plan. As far as the main part of *Ark Royal*'s ship's company was concerned it was a return trip to their old friend the Regia Aeronautica at Gagliari.

On 9th November they blitzed Gagliari. The ride was a great deal rougher this time. The Italians had built up their anti-aircraft defences to formidable strength. Swordfish returned to the *Ark* after bombing hangars and a factory with the scars from a hundred guns in wings and fuselage.

They were out for five days on this job, and when they returned to Gibraltar – to find the beer boat had come and gone, and the Army had drunk the lot – they were told that torpedo squadrons from the *Illustrious* had attacked the Italian Battle Fleet in Taranto Harbour and put half the enemy fleet out of action.

Some of them were annoyed that they had only been used as a diversion. They felt that the old *Ark*, as the senior ship and the Navy's most famous carrier, should have been given the honour of Taranto. But their effort had materially helped the success of the whole complex plan known as M.B.8, a combined operation covering convoys to Greece (which were now being heavily attacked by the Italians), to Crete, and to Malta, of which part was formed by Operation Coat (a movement of reinforcements to the fleet), part by Operation Crack (*Ark Royal*'s attack, which covered the latter), and part by Operation Judgment (*Illustrious*'s attack on Taranto). So everyone who took part in M.B.8 had a share in the signal victory which really put the bombers of the Fleet Air Arm in their rightful place as a great war-winning weapon. On their way to Cagliari the new Fulmars, which everyone agreed were delightful aircraft to fly, scored their first victory, a Savoia 79, and next day Fulmars and Skuas together shot down a Cant and another Savoia.

From now on the new fighters of 808 were in continuous action, providing air cover and combat air patrols, and generally defending the fleet and the convoys that passed through the Mediterranean from west to east. It was a period during which the British forces in the Mediterranean gradually dominated the Italians on land, on sea, and in the air.

The *Ark* and Force H now faced a long, hard winter of maximum effort. A pattern slowly grew of long days at sea and weary hours in the air, of short, fierce dogfights over the fleet, and brief, warm hours ashore on the Rock. There is nothing in the world more wearisome, more demanding of a man, that watch-keeping at sea in action. Four hours on – at the guns, straining the eyes over sea and sky for signs of the enemy, with periods of acute concentration and effort when he does come, down in the magazines in the half-light with the nerve-racking clangour of battle ebbing and flowing somewhere far away, in the engine-room tending that vital machinery with red-eyed constant alertness. Then four hours of uneasy rest, liable to be broken at any minute by a shrill, nerve-jangling call to action stations which might last all day and night and find you facing at the end of it your turn for another four hours on watch. It is worse, in a way, than the actual battle, because it is more insidious, and a bigger, more drawn-out test of a man – of his nerves, then his concentration and ability, and at last the basic stuff of which he was made, which alone can carry him through all this endless purgatory.

The new naval air mechanics found their routine very hard for a while. Their work consisted mainly of the maintenance of the aircraft, with domestic duties like 'cook of the mess' and an occasional turn at storing ship thrown in.

An inspection of the aircraft was carried out daily whenever there was flying. Before a Fulmar flew she was checked to see that all her controls worked and that any damage had been repaired, that she was full of fuel, oil, and coolant, and there were no leaks anywhere. The armourers saw to it that the ammunition was in the stowages and the guns loaded. Sometimes someone would make an unintentional functional check of the loaded guns. Everyone in the hangar would immediately fly wildly to shelter or hurl themselves to the deck. Once a bulkhead got thoroughly peppered, and men standing on the weather-deck on the other side of it had to spend some weeks in sick bay.

It was rather like running a big garage, except that here every machine had to be thoroughly checked, not every thousand miles, but every thirty hours. Vital parts were completely dismantled then, sparking plugs, oil and coolant changed, oil systems flushed, fuel, oil, and hydraulics checked, and the guns stripped right down

127

and thoroughly cleaned. This inspection together with aircraft compass swinging and gun alignment, took up much of their time when the ship was in harbour.

While the mechanics were working flat out ashore on the aircraft the ordnance men slaved on the guns. Often each gun fired anything from fifty to seventy rounds during a prolonged air attack, and back in harbour they had to be stripped, cleaned, and thoroughly examined, repairs effected, and every gun brought to a state of readiness for action. All the gun barrels of the 4.5's had to be changed after they had fired an allotted number of rounds. This meant working day and night in shifts until all sixteen barrels had been changed.

As a direct result of the victory at Taranto it was decided that it would now be comparatively safe to send a convoy through the Mediterranean from west to east, comprising two transports for Malta and one for Alexandria. Force H, *Renown*, *Ark Royal*, *Sheffield*, *Despatch*, and nine destroyers, together with a close-escort force, was to escort the merchantmen to a position south of Sardinia, where they would be joined by *Ramillies*, *Newcastle*, *Berwick*, *Coventry*, and five destroyers from the Mediterranean Fleet. When the dangerous passage of the narrows south of Sicily had been made under cover of darkness, Force H, with *Ramillies*, *Newcastle*, and *Berwick*, would then return to Gibraltar, and the remainder would steer for Malta, meeting the rest of the Mediterranean Fleet next day.

For a time there was no sign of the enemy, but at 6.30 a.m. on 27th November a force of battleships, cruisers, and destroyers was sighted off the southern point of Sardinia, Cape Spartivento, first by aircraft from Malta, and a little later by a Swordfish from *Ark Royal* herself. A second Swordfish from the *Ark*, dodging from cloud to cloud, held on to the enemy and reported his movements as Force H turned into line of battle, guardrails down, battle ensigns flying. At 11.30 a.m. they turned towards the enemy, the cruisers leading.

Soon afterwards the *Ramillies* and her squadron joined them.

Ark Royal flew off a striking force of eleven bombers from 810 Squadron to try to slow the Italian force down, which had by now been identified as the battleships *Vittorio Veneto* and *Guilio Cesare*, seven heavy cruisers, and sixteen destroyers. They disappeared into the blue emptiness of the sky towards Spartivento.

At 12.20 our leading ships opened fire on the western-most Italian cruisers, but the Italian admiral had signalled them not to be drawn into a battle, and they retired towards their battleships under a smoke-screen. The fight continued at long range. At 12.40 the Italian battleships sighted the bombers from *Ark Royal*.

'It was one of those clear, brittle Mediterranean days,' wrote one of our observers, 'the sun shining in a cloudless sky, the sea as smooth as a piece of satin. The striking force had as little cover as a battalion marching across a meadow.'

Out of this bare, brilliant sky the eleven machines dived towards the *Vittorio Veneto*. Pilots thrust in through the burning, stinking flak and claimed two hits, airgunners shattered the windows of the flagship's bridge.

But the force was too small to do any vital damage. They failed to slow the Italians. By now Admiral Somerville felt that he could put no further distance between his forces and the convoy which they had temporarily left behind, especially since the most dangerous part of the passage lay immediately ahead, and at 1.12 he broke off the chase.

Shortly afterwards he received a report that an Italian cruiser lay damaged near the Sardinian coast. A wave of nine machines was ordered up from *Ark Royal* to attack her, and the other fleeing units of the Italian squadron. They failed to find the damaged ship, but attacked other cruisers which they found steering north along the Sardinian coast. They hit one ship, and a geyser

9

of boiling smoke and spray shot up as high as her bridge. They also claimed another cruiser hit and slowed down. Then they had to return to the carrier. Once again they had attacked with great courage and determination, but, alas, were far too few. Given a hundred planes instead of twenty, five carriers instead of one, the Fleet Air Arm might well have sunk many of the enemy ships, or at least slowed them down for our big guns to engage. 'Give us more carriers!' was their cri de coeur. However, the convoy was passed safely through.

It was always the same. The enemy had the numbers. That day massed squadrons of bombers came over Force H when *Ark Royal* was steaming alone, operating aircraft, three miles away from the other ships. Admiral Somerville, watching from the *Renown,* thought she had gone. Then her big blunt nosed poked angrily out of the smoke again, her guns blazing.

On this and all such occasions the carrier-borne fighters kept up a shield over the fleet. A shadowing Cant or Savoia which came too close had very little chance of survival, and the enemy's massed squadrons of high-level bombers missed their targets again and again because of the fighters' persistent attacks, usually returning to their airfields in Sardinia and Sicily with one or two machines short and others limping badly.

The Fulmars, though delightful machines to fly, were not nearly so fast or so manoeuvrable as Hurricanes or Spitfires, and they frequently had to dogfight with the much faster Macchis and the exceptionally agile little C.R.42's, but their pilots learned, by experience and by constant dummy dogfights amongst themselves, to use them to the best advantage. It is amazing to think that there were only a dozen of them at this stage in the entire Mediterranean. In anything like large numbers there is no knowing what destruction they might not have wrought. As for the hope of anything better than the Fulmar, there was none at this time. It was still thought impossible to operate Hurricanes, let alone Spitfires, from the carriers, and no-one had tried yet. All the best fighters continued to go to the R.A.F. at home. Even Malta, whose need for Hurricanes was ever desperate, could only get them in small batches.

It was to be hoped that this state of affairs would improve in the very near future, because by the end of the year there were increasing signs that the Fulmars would soon be fighting something worse than C.R.42's.

CHAPTER VII

FIND, FIX AND STRIKE

In April 1941 a young R.N.V.R. fighter pilot, Lieutenant R. E. Gardner, joined the *Ark Royal*. In his log-book was written in brief, laconic entries, a small epic of the Royal Navy's war in the air. From his earliest entry it ran:

Total hours flown before 2.9.39 = 340

Cross-country flights:

        Dyce – Le Tourquet – Zurich – Stockholm
        Bangor – Le Bourget – Basle – Copenhagen
        Bircham Newton – Dinard – Berlin
        St Eval – Lyons – Hamburg
        Ramsgate – Marseilles.

29.8.39	Interview at the Admiralty.
2.9.39	Flight test at Lee-on-Solent, R.N.A.S.
7.9.39	Posted Eastleigh 780 Squadron, R.N.
July 1940	With 242 Squadron R.A.F. under S/Ldr Douglas Bader on first operational flight in Hurricane 1 – 1 Heinkel

	III Mk V destroyed 40 miles S.E. of Yarmouth after 3 quarter to stern attacks.
August 1940	1 Dornier 215 destroyed 20 miles south of Norwich. 1 stern attack.
September 1940	1 Ju 88 destroyed Shell Haven, Essex. 1 stern attack.
October 1940	1 Ju 88 and 1 Dornier 215 destroyed East London.
November 1940	Shot down by Me 109. Clot!
May 8th, 1941	With 807 Squadron R.N. under Lieutenant-Commander Sholto Douglas in Fulmar aircraft. Embarked in H.M.S. *Ark Royal*.

The German blitz was like a huge amoeba. Sprawling over Europe its fluid shape assumed long arms of assault, fire-tipped with air power, wherever the strategy of her lightning war directed.

When they had overwhelmed France, one of these arms jumped the Channel and tried to absorb Britain also. It stubbed its fury on Fighter Command. So the arm withdrew and the amoeba had to change its shape again. This time, instead of assaulting us direct, it began the longer job of encircling us first, of overcoming us abroad and starving us at home. The squadrons of bombers and fighters which had been poured to no avail into the Battle of Britain were switched elsewhere to spearhead the armoured tide, to lead great attacks by German armies upon the scattered Allied forces, and by the German Navy's powerful U-boat and surface raiders against the merchant ships that fed our resistance.

Hitler had not bargained for this deployment of his forces. He had hoped to crush Britain first, then turn with all his strength upon Russia, but when plans for a September invasion of Britain had to be cancelled, the Germans commenced the new strategy. In October the *Admiral Scheer* left Germany and began a raiding cruise. On 5th November she sank the gallant *Jervis Bay* and five other ships of her convoy, then went on to sink eight more merchantmen in the South Atlantic and Indian Ocean.

In October, also, the Germans moved into Rumania to secure the Rumanian oil-fields, establish a southern buttress for the attack on Russia, and to pave the way for a great drive on the Middle East through the Balkans. The first essential in this great plan was the occupation of Greece. This would both protect Rumanian oil from British bombers, and further the drive on Egypt. The second essential was defeat of the British Army in North Africa under General Wavell, so that Egypt would be threatened on that side as well.

But on 28th October the Italians invaded Greece of their own accord, without consulting Germany. They came up against fierce resistance from the Greek Army and began to get the worst of it.

Then, just before Christmas, General Wavell soundly thrashed the Italians in North Africa and began to drive them back.

In the same month the eight-inch cruiser *Admiral Hipper* came out from Germany and began to look for our convoys.

Force H at Gibraltar had planned a bumper Christmas. Aboard *Ark Royal* a special concert had been organised. On Christmas Day the messes were gaily decorated with bunting. The captain made the customary tour of inspection to pick out the best-decorated mess, and wished the ship's company a Happy Christmas. Christmas cheer had been drunk and everyone was tucking into the turkey when the commander announced that they were to put to sea immediately.

The *Hipper* had spoiled their Christmas. Down came the decorations and away went the duty watch. The German cruiser had been reported in action with the cruisers *Berwick* and *Bonaventure*, which were escorting a Suez-bound convoy about three hundred miles north-east of

the Azores. After a short fight the *Hipper* made o[...]
the protection of poor visibility and contact w[...]
with her.

Ark Royal put out and tried to find her, but [...] no
luck. Eventually she escorted the damaged *Berwick* back
into Gibraltar. There she waited to see what the year
1941 would bring.

It brought the Germans in greater and greater
strength. The Luftwaffe came to the Mediterranean to
support the new German Army which General Rommel
was organising in North Africa, to give him direct co-
operation over the battlefields, to sink the ships bringing
supplies and reinforcements to General Wavell, to smash
Malta, the 'unsinkable aircraft-carrier' which had been
contributing so much to the Italian failure in North
Africa, and to knock out the more mobile aircraft-
carriers of the fleet, specially *Ark Royal* and *Illustrious*.

The Axis owed these two ships a bitter grudge. They,
more than any other ship in the fleet, had contributed
to the state of affairs which now forced the Nazis to send
men and machines which were really needed to attack
Russia to the Mediterranean theatre. The aeroplanes
from the two carriers had helped to ruin and demoralise
the Italians throughout the summer and fall of 1940.
Ark Royal had beaten off the Regia Aeronautica from
our ships, and thus helped Wavell to inflict a humiliating
defeat upon the Italian Army. *Illustrious* had knocked
out half the Italian Battle Fleet at Taranto.

In accomplishing all this they had brought the Luftwaffe against them. In January 1941 the Nazi 10th Air
Corps moved into Sicily to dominate the scene.

Illustrious's fighters saw them first. Early in January
Operation Excess was organised to send a convoy
through to Malta. Force H, comprising *Ark Royal*,
Renown, *Malaya*, *Sheffield*, and seven destroyers,
escorted it through their parish, then the main fleet took
over. *Illustrious* was steaming with the convoy in the
Sicilian Channel when she was heavily attacked by the

newly arrived German bombers. Crippled and listing, she just managed to reach Malta. After emerging comparatively unscathed from a series of vicious attacks in Grand Harbour, she eventually managed to get away to Alexandria, and, subsequently, to the United States, where she was repaired.

That left the *Ark Royal* alone again for a while, but she was used to that. She often headed west into the Atlantic as well, to protect outward- and homeward-bound convoys. The fear that more German raiders would attack our merchantmen in the Atlantic was causing the Admiralty great anxiety. Their fears were to be proved amply justified. The *Hipper* had sunk a merchantman just after her encounter with the *Berwick* on Christmas Day, then had made for Brest before *Ark Royal*'s aircraft could catch up with her. In February she came out again, and on the 12th attacked a slow, unescorted Sierra Leone convoy, sinking seven ships before a merciful mist allowed the rest to escape.

But a worse threat than the *Hipper* loomed. *Scharnhorst* and *Gneisenau* were out. Early in February they slipped out into the Atlantic south of Iceland, eluding a patrolling armed merchant cruiser by the use of radar. On 8th February they sighted a convoy coming in from Canada, and only sheered off when they saw the battleship *Ramillies*. Then on the 22nd February they sank five ships which had been dispersed from an outward-bound convoy and were sailing on their own.

Ark Royal knew they were out, and always hoped for a chance to strike at her old enemies and finally avenge the *Glorious*. Force H had to keep a particularly watchful eye upon the movements of these powerful ships, for the Admiralty feared that the Germans might attempt at any time to send one or more of them through into the Mediterranean to stiffen the Italian resistance as the *Goeben* and *Breslau* had done for the Turks in the first Great War, and provide a very dangerous threat to our shipping there. Their anxiety on this score increased as it became obvious that the two new German battleships *Bismarck* and *Tirpitz*, the most powerful warships in the world, were ready to make their maiden cruises. Perhaps one or more of these great ships would try to break through and give support to the German drive on the Middle East. Perhaps an even greater blow was planned, with German battleships, battlecruisers, and heavy cruisers acting together. As March came in the situation became more fraught with anxiety. It was the month of decision. Rommel's army was poised in North Africa, another in the Balkans. U-boats and E-boats were attacking our shipping, *Scharnhorst* and *Gneisenau* were somewhere at sea, *Bismarck* and *Tirpitz* were ready to sail, and the Italian Air Force and Battle Fleet, roused to action by German pressure and the example set them by the Luftwaffe, were becoming more belligerent.

As a result *Ark Royal*'s aircraft had been busy since the opening of the new year. The Fulmars saw plenty of action and shot down a number of Italian bombers. But the Italian torpedo-bomber pilots were brave and skilful and gave the gunners and fighter pilots of the *Ark* many tense moments.

First signs of the enemy would appear on the second day out from Gibraltar in the shape of a shadower, usually one of their Cant 506B seaplanes, big, cumbersome machines, possessing, however, a long operational range and endurance. The Cants were easy to deal with if the Fulmars could get within striking distance, but they became very wary. If our fighters were already up over the fleet they kept at a safe distance. If they were not, the Italian aircrews kept a very watchful eye on the *Ark Royal*, and as soon as they saw aircraft taking off pointed their noses for home and were out of range before the fighters had a chance to engage them. The Fulmars on the other hand always tried to get to them before they had time to send their reports of the convoy's position, course and speed back to the airfields where their bombers were waiting for the word to take off.

Fighter direction technique in Force H was rudimentary at this stage. The *Sheffield* had radar, *Ark Royal* had not, so the cruiser would always lie astern of the carrier and pass the positions of approaching enemy aircraft to her by morse. These were plotted in the *Ark*, which then directed her fighters to the enemy. Radio communications too were unsatisfactory, and there was bound to be an unfortunate time-lag in the interception of the enemy. Lieutenant-Commander Coke, *Ark*'s Fighter Direction Officer during many of these engagements, cut this to a minimum by doing all the fighter direction himself. He would sit with a plotting board on his knee, listening to the *Sheffield* and talking to the fighters at the same time. It was not a method which could easily be copied, unfortunately, as Coke was a virtuoso.

The Fulmars were slow machines, and some were lost dogfighting the fast, agile C.R.42's. As the year wore on they began to see more and more Messerschmitts, and things became even more dangerous and difficult for them. It was worst of all for the men in the back seats. They had nothing at all with which to defend themselves, all the guns in the Fulmar being forward firing. One day when O'Nion was stretching his legs in Gibraltar he bought a camera, with the idea of taking it up in the air with him and snapping some action shots. He was an enthusiastic amateur photographer, and he also felt that anything which could be held in the hands and pointed at the enemy might inspire confidence.

Three of them were on combat air patrol one day when a report came in of a shadower. Cloud level was low and very thick, and the three Fulmars separated to search the area. As O'Nion's pilot, Petty Officer 'Buck' Taylor, came round the side of a cloud, round from the other side appeared the shadower, a Cant 506. It was so close that O'Nion could see the pilot in his cockpit and the rear-gunner in his turret.

The Italian immediately sheered off, and Taylor did

138

a flick turn on to his tail, losing him for a moment as they both plunged into thick cloud. When they came out the Fulmar opened up with its eight guns and bits started to fly off the Cant, which quickly went into a steep dive and force-landed on the sea.

O'Nion suddenly remembered his camera and asked Taylor to go down low and circle round the seaplane. All the crew of the Cant except the rear-gunner, who was lying half in, half out of his turret, were inflating their rubber dinghy. O'Nion took several shots, and a report was sent to Force H by the broadcast system, by which a general message could be passed over the air, requiring no answer from anyone, and thus not betraying the position. The Italian crew were picked up later, and O'Nion returned to the ship, where his photographs were developed. They came out beautifully, and were immediately sent to the admiral.

The telegraphist-air-gunners had no guns, but they did what they could to throw things at the enemy. They used to tear up rolls of toilet paper and make them into bundles tied up with elastic bands. When an enemy fighter got on his tail the T.A.G. would open the cockpit hood, whip the band off, and heave the bundle out into the slipstream. The enemy often thought the shower of white confetti was a secret weapon and sheered off. Later on they were provided with tommy-guns, but their low velocity made them useless in the air.

Lieutenant-Commander Tillard, the C.O. of 808 Squadron, was an inspiration. He led many successful combats. Once he attacked two Savoias single-handed so that the rest of the squadron could deal unhampered with the main attack on the fleet. He came in from astern of the rear machine and closed in, firing, to two hundred yards. The Savoia caught fire and exploded, and he turned to the second one, which he shot down on fire into the sea from a range of a hundred and seventy yards.

The Swordfish saw plenty of action, too. On 2nd

February they took off and attacked the Tirso dam in Sardinia. They took off in foul weather before first light, with *Ark Royal*'s deck heaving and pitching, and flew through buffeting head-winds and torrential rain and hail to the Sardinian coast. It was still dark and very cloudy, and ice had begun to form on their wings. When they reached their target the barrage was intense and only four of the eight machines managed to launch their torpedoes against the dam.

A week later they took off once more, eighteen aircraft with torpedoes and mines, in the darkness to attack the great Azienda oil refinery in Leghorn, while the rest of Force H bombarded Genoa and Spezia.

It was one of the first real strategical bombing missions by carrier-borne forces, and once more the *Ark Royal* demonstrated the superior mobility of the carrier as a weapon. Striking swiftly from sea they were able to choose the time and place of their attack and achieve complete surprise. The Italians were entirely unprepared, and the striking force was able to blast the refinery with high explosive and incendiary practically without opposition.

The Navy struck hard at the Italians throughout February all over the Mediterranean, clearing the way for our convoys. It was now obvious that a German invasion of Greece was imminent, so it was decided that over half of General Wavell's army must be transported there. Convoys began early in March to take the troops across to Greece from Egypt.

The Mediterranean Fleet covered all these convoys, and on 27th March came in contact with the Italian Battle Fleet off Cape Matapan. Fleet Air Arm torpedo bombers from Crete and from the *Formidable*, which had relieved the *Illustrious*, played a big part in the resounding victory which Admiral Cunningham achieved.

But three days after Matapan, Rommel's army began to attack Wavell's now seriously depleted force in the Western Desert and drive it back towards the Nile. Almost simultaneously the German Army and the Luftwaffe began to smash their way down through Greece.

Out in the Atlantic the old firm of *Scharnhorst* and *Gneisenau* was active again. Cruising between the Canaries and the Cape Verde Islands on 7th-8th March they sighted a homeward-bound British convoy. When they saw the battleship *Malaya* they thought better of attacking the convoy themselves, but directed a U-boat pack on to it which sank five of its ships. A week later the two battlecruisers attacked a weak convoy in mid-Atlantic and sank sixteen ships before the *Rodney* came up and they made off.

These two fast, powerful ships were a much greater menace to our merchantmen than the pocket battleships, and their activities were causing the Admiralty grave concern. They called up all the ships that could be spared to hunt for them, among these the *Ark Royal* and *Renown* from Gibraltar. At 5.30 p.m. on 20th March one of *Ark*'s Fulmars sighted *Scharnhorst* and *Gneisenau* at extreme range in bad visibility about six hundred miles west-nor-west of Finisterre. As soon as the observer tried to send his report back to Force H his wireless broke down. They would have to go all the way, about a hundred and sixty miles, back to the force before Admiral Somerville could be informed.

Meanwhile the Germans had seen them. Admiral Lütjens in *Scharnhorst* immediately turned from his north-easterly course to due north, and, when the shadower disappeared, turned back north-east again, to try and throw any pursuit off the scent. When the Fulmar regained Force H the observer first contacted *Renown* and signalled that the German ships had last been seen heading due north. It was not until he returned to *Ark Royal* that he remembered to say that the enemy had, when first sighted, been steering north-east. Somerville was therefore given no chance to spot Lütjen's ruse. To make matters worse *Ark Royal* had become separated from the flagship, and was twenty miles away from her when the Fulmar landed-on, with the result that Somerville did not receive the additional information until some hours later. Those hours were spent by Force H steaming at full speed trying hard to close the gap sufficiently for a striking force to be flown off the carrier to catch the battlecruisers and slow them down with torpedoes. While Force H tried to close the enemy it was essential to find him again and maintain contact with him. Here the weather was against them, and bad visibility prevented any possibility of shadowing at night. The weather was just as bad the next morning, and the hunt was subsequently abandoned. 'It was extremely unlucky,' said Somerville, 'that we did not sight them earlier in the afternoon. Goodness knows how many thousands of miles the boys have flown looking for those two ships.'

After this disappointing chase Force H returned to Gibraltar, and *Ark Royal* prepared to go east again, this time into the Mediterranean with air support for our ships. Her men took the opportunity of relaxing ashore and enjoying themselves while they could. A big attraction about this time was the visit of Paca Romero, a once-famous Spanish dancer, and her troupe. They appeared at the theatre for two weeks, and many sailors from the *Ark* went again and again, mainly to watch a young Spanish dancer and singer named Victoria Madrid. Later on the troupe came on board the carrier and put on a show on a stage especially rigged up under the flight-deck pom-poms. So exotic and glamorous on the stage, what a pathetic, half-starved crowd they seemed at close quarters!

Church services on board in the hangar were always crowded, and the lovely chapel was used regularly for communion. At times the Naafi shop on board ran right out of chocolate. Then it was a question of,

'Any nutty?'

'Sorry, only gums.'

'You must have bloody shares in Rowntrees!'

Force H had by this time become something of a

142

legend. All new ships which passed through the Mediterranean from 'our end', as Force H called it, to the east were always greeted with the signal,

'Welcome to the Force H Club!'

The force did so much sea-time, both in the Mediterranean and the Atlantic, that once Admiral Somerville signalled,

'It is quite possible that in the next fortnight members of the club will be able to have a night in their hammocks.'

That did not happen very often, with commerce raiders in the Atlantic and Italian airfields full of Messerschmitts and Stukas. But there was never any panic when the *Ark* was in Bomb Alley. This happy indifference amazed young matelots like Claydon. His action station was down in a gunnery transmitting station. It was always unbearably hot down there, especially as all the fans were turned off during an action, and all any of them wore was a pair of shorts and slippers. During lulls they used to play 'uckers', and the only concern Claydon ever saw anyone show was when another attack forced them to abandon the game. Sometimes an Italian bomber would sneak up during a 'relax action stations' period and drop a few bombs, always planting at least one near the ventilator entrance so that the fans sucked in the fumes and poisoned the air down there a little more.

The ships' cooks were always kept busy making countless sandwiches, sausage rolls, and pasties for the ship's company to eat on watch. At one time during a club run, when the action lasted longer than usual, the galley was full of an odd assortment of people all taking advantage of a momentary lull to make sandwiches. The paymaster commander himself was turning the handle of the bacon machine, slicing up the bread. There was always this sort of wonderful team spirit everywhere.

Despite the huge concrete catchments, the Rock used to run short of water, and the *Ark*, which made her own

143

fresh water, was called upon from time to time to help. There was another occasion when an iron lung was urgently required at the military hospital. Under the personal supervision of the ship's surgeons the *Ark*'s shipwrights worked unceasingly into the night to make one from timber and rubber sheeting. It became the custom to give soldiers at Gibraltar a 'holiday' by taking small parties of them to sea on operational trips. Most of them seemed very glad to get back. One or two of them were even given joy rides in the air, although this practice was stopped when one soldier passenger was discovered on landing to have died in the air.

Once they took on board a squadron of Swordfish which had been operating in the desert. One of these, called 'Desert Rat', was being catapulted off armed with depth charges when she suddenly crumpled up and disappeared over the bows. Her depth-charges went off under water at the required depth, and almost blew the *Ark* out of the water. Mechanics in the hangar at the time saw some aircraft rise about a foot on their oleo legs, and some rise completely clear of the deck. Those below thought it was the end. Kenneth Lord was having a shower at the time, and rushed up on deck stark naked, fully prepared to abandon ship just as he was.

On 19th April Captain L. E. H. Maund relieved Captain Holland in command of *Ark Royal*. Maund had been a cruiser man, having come back from the Far East in the *Danae* just before the war. The First Sea Lord had promised him an early sea-going command, but he had had to wait until now to fulfil his life-long ambition as a sailor. The intervening period he had spent in the working-up and organisation of Combined Operations. He had enjoyed the work, but longed all the time for a ship. At Narvik he had gone in with the Expeditionary Force, and had often watched the fighters from the *Ark Royal* overhead with a feeling of intense service pride. Now he commanded that great and famous ship. He was back with the frigates again, for that was what the *Ark* really was, a cruiser-carrier, fast, lightly built and armoured.

For the operation which was now on hand, the passage of five fast merchant ships to Alexandria, Admiral Somerville could really have done with a more heavily armoured ship like the *Formidable* down in the 'man's end' of the Mediterranean. He feared the loss of such a valuable ship as the *Ark*, with her expert air group, at this stage in the war. *Ark Royal*'s flight-deck was un-armoured. Remembering what a German dive-bomber's thousand pounder had done to *Illustrious*, for all her armour, he thought of the fatal havoc such a bomb, ripping through *Ark*'s thin flying-deck like paper and exploding among aircraft fuelling below, could do. *Illustrious* had only just managed to survive. For *Ark Royal* it might mean the end.

A carrier's best protection against dive-bombers was her own fighters. Here, Admiral Somerville felt, was the gravest cause for alarm, for *Ark* had only eleven Ful-mars fit to take the air – eleven slow, cumbersome, con-verted light bombers to keep off Me.109's and 110's, C.R. 42's, Stukas and Heinkel V's. But Malta was in desperate straits, and the convoy must get through at all costs, even at the risk of losing the *Ark*, so she went after all.

The convoy was sent through the Straits of Gibraltar during the night of 6th-7th May, while the convoy escorts were fuelled in Gibraltar. By dawn all the ships were out of sight of land. Force H, *Renown*, *Sheffield*, *Ark Royal*, and their destroyers, steamed on ahead of the convoy and its close escort to try and draw the attention of Italian reconnaissance planes. Beyond the routine Sword-fish anti-submarine patrol there was no flying on the first day. Italian submarines were known to patrol the area in the path of a convoy, but they had strict orders not to engage a heavily escorted force, although they could easily surface after it had passed over them and radio its position.

It was on 7th May that signs of trouble started. Gradually the horizon stirred with hostile life. Snoopers were reported by *Sheffield*'s radar, and *Ark*'s Fulmars went up after them and drove them away.

On the following day the storm broke. At dawn Force H regained the convoy to protect the merchant ships at this, the most dangerous stage of the voyage.

Between 7 and 8 a.m. they intercepted the first enemy reports of the convoy and knew they could expect attacks in an hour or so. By that time the eleven Fulmars must be in the sky waiting to pounce. The moment would be difficult to anticipate. Whatever happened, the slow-climbing Fulmars must not be caught on deck, least of all down in the hangar refuelling. The direction and strength of the wind, too, ever fickle, could make the vital difference between getting fighters airborne in time or too late. Everything had to be gauged to a nicety.

When the enemy appeared, however, the little band of Fulmars was up and ready, and hurled themselves upon him. Early in the battle 808 Squadron lost its gallant commanding officer and senior observer, both of whom had won the D.S.C. in the *Ark*. Tillard and Somerville, seeing three C.R.42 fighters below them, dived and flew at them head on. But the cumbersome Fulmar was no match for three of the slippery little Fiats in able hands, and the Fulmar was last seen going down towards the sea. They were never heard of again. It was a sad blow for the Flag Officer, Force H, for Lieutenant Somerville was his nephew, and a heavy loss for *Ark Royal*.

Enemy attacks continued all through the day. By 7 p.m. the Fulmars were down to seven in number. It was at this stage that a report came in of over forty dive-bombers approaching from Sicily. 'It was,' Captain Maund said later, 'the only occasion on which I remember feeling at all uncertain. . . . That meant a determined German attack, and we had little doubt which of us would be the target.

'There was a great cloud to our northward rising from

1,000 feet to 10,000 feet, while overhead it was bright clear sky. The dive-bombers made their way westward out of sight behind and above the cloud. As the seven popped through the fringe we were surprised to see some big splashes under the cloud to our northward. We could not believe the good news. The dive-bombers thought the Fulmars were Hurricanes; they knew they could not compete with a Hurricane so they jettisoned their bombs and dived down into the cloud for safety, but not before the seven had shot one of them down and winged another.'

The enemy formation included twenty-eight Junkers 87's and an escort of Me.110's. The Fulmars thrust in amongst them and several of the Messerschmitts as well as the more unwieldy Stukas were destroyed, others being sent limping back to Sicily, some to crash into the sea before they could regain their airfields.

There were further torpedo and bombing attacks that day, and the final one was made by four torpedo bombers. Three Fulmars, all that could be made airworthy by now, scattered them and shot down the leader.

When the fighting was over Lieutenant Gardner wrote in his log, after the entries recording his days with Douglas Bader when he had first learned how to deal with Germans:

    1 Savoia 79 shared with Lt. Firth
    1 Savoia 79 attacked. Lost in cloud.
    1 Ju 87 destroyed
    1 Ju 87 probable. (Confirmed by cine-camera)
    Force-landed on H.M.S. *Ark Royal*.

He led four sorties against the Luftwaffe and Italians that day. On his last attack he was leading a section of three Fulmars when he saw a number of Stukas below him heading in the opposite direction. Swiftly he dived to head them off. As he was making his attack the windscreen in front of him suddenly cracked into frosty opaqueness, hit by a German bullet. He could still see, and tried desperately to engage the Germans, but by the time he was ready to attack he had lost them. His Fulmar had been badly damaged, and he only just managed to regain *Ark Royal* and crash-land aboard.

For Leading-Airman Orme it was his first combat. When his pilot attacked a bunch of C.R.42's he kept them both alive by shouting warnings of impending attacks, keeping it up even when the Italians forced them down out of control. Helpless to hit back himself, Orme opened the hood and hurled the faithful bundle of toilet paper at their attackers. Twice he made them break off in this way.

Another rating observer, Petty Officer L. G. J. Howard, became involved in a fierce encounter with Italian fighters, and had this to say about the action afterwards:

'I was on patrol with a section at about ten in the morning when we spotted a single aircraft well below us. We dived to attack, and hit him quite hard, and he went into a steep spin. Although I did not see him hit the sea I should be very surprised if he ever pulled out of that spin. Before we could pull up and regain formation, the C.R.42's were on us. I counted at least five. They seemed to come at us from all directions, and I was kept busy trying to tell the pilot where they were. Several bullets hit the aircraft, and one particularly persistent Italian gentleman would stay on our tail. We had evolved a remarkably successful method of shaking off anyone on our tail simply by letting go in the slip-stream a hand-ful of Admiralty pattern toilet paper which we kept in the back cockpit, the theory being that the chap following seeing something coming back at him thought it was pieces of the aircraft he was attacking, and he got out of the way quickly. This dodge had worked on several occasions, and I was in the act of reaching for the paper when I was hit in the leg. I remember no sensation of great pain, and think I said "My God" or something like that

over the inter-com. I was able to tell the pil[ot]
what had happened when he enquired if I had [been hit].
We eventually shook off our pursuers, and [we]
requested permission to return to base reporting [I]
had been wounded.

'I remember quite distinctly on the way back trying
to staunch the flow of blood with a handkerchief, and
being rather amused at watching the lower half of my
leg flapping idly about. We saw several Italian torpedo
aircraft in the sea as we came to land-on. A very determined torpedo attack had been made, but without
success.

'I was whipped out of the aircraft in the hangar and
down to the emergency operating theatre where Surgeon-
Commander Williams and his assistants performed an
emergency operation which probably saved me from
losing my leg. I had been hit by an explosive bullet which
had exploded inside my leg completely shattering both
tibia and fibula. I woke from the anaesthetic that evening
to the sound of gunfire; the last attack of a continuous
succession that day was being repulsed.'

For everyone it was sweat and toil unending that day,
especially for the flight-deck personnel, the ground-crews
in the hangars, and the engine-room staff. For the mechanics working frantically on each Fulmar as it came
down in the lift to patch it up and fill it with fuel again
for the next sortie, and for the stokers, ammunition
parties, and engineers, the pace was so furious that there
was no time to think of the bomb which might at any
moment rip open the deckhead and blow the hangar into
blazing ruin, and the whole ship into a petrol-soaked,
exploding hulk. The few Fulmars left at the end of the
day were all in need of repair. All kinds of vital components were changed in the heat of battle. Once a whole
undercarriage was removed and a new one fitted. Bullet-
riddled propellers were replaced. One pilot blanched
somewhat when a mechanic dug out bullets from the
priming pump next to his left thigh. Hurried first aid

was done by putting fabric patches over jagged holes in the metal wings and fuselages. There was only one machine which the sweating ground-crews could not put right in time to go up and fight again. That one had bullet holes in the crankcase of the engine.

Thanks largely to their efforts, and to the heroic work of the Fulmars, Operation Tiger was successfully achieved, although one transport carrying more than a quarter of the tanks for Wavell was sunk by a mine. At the same time Admiral Cunningham received reinforcements consisting of the battleship *Queen Elizabeth* and two cruisers.

He was going to need them. This was the last through convoy for two years. From this point on the Germans really began to apply the pressure. They were in a hurry, for they planned to attack Russia within the next few weeks, and wanted badly to consolidate their southern boundary in the Mediterranean and push it as far away from Rumania and the Russian border as possible, at the same time driving towards a junction with Rommel in Egypt.

On 20th May they began the invasion of Crete, and the Mediterranean Fleet found itself fully committed to one of the hardest, cruellest struggles in the history of the Royal Navy.

In the western Mediterranean the atmosphere became the quieter for the hurricane raging in the East, which had sucked in Admiral Cunningham's ships and General Geissler's dive-bombers from Sicily alike.

But as the airborne onslaught on Crete began came fearful danger to our shipping from west of Gibraltar.

The *Bismarck* was out.

Admiral Somerville received the news on 23rd May that she and *Prinz Eugen* were heading into the Atlantic, having broken out of Bergen. He was ordered to sail at once for the Bay of Biscay.

Ark Royal sailed at 2 a.m. Tugs hauled her off the wall, then she slid silent and huge out past the sleeping ships. Admiral Somerville in *Renown* strained his eyes to see her. Often he had said,

'If I haven't got the *Ark* with me I feel like a blind beggar without his dog.'

In the anxious hours ahead he would need her more than ever. *Renown* was no match for *Bismarck*. She was old, out-gunned, and thinly armoured, and her hull was in need of repair. All the ships of Force H showed the signs of hard campaigning. *Ark Royal* herself had steamed 100,000 miles, and needed a major refit. The two aircraft depth-charges which had exploded underneath her some months before had badly dented her hull. Captain Maund had to keep a shipwright at work every day at sea caulking and welding loose rivets and cracks in her plates, and the tremendous vibration from her well-worn propeller shafts made matters worse. Twice, in fact, the stern gland of the centre shaft had blown out.

It was to be hoped that it did not blow out again with the *Bismarck* close at hand. The engineers were on their toes as always, ready for trouble. Repairs were sometimes actually being done below when *Ark* received an urgent order to raise steam for leaving harbour. But somehow she always made it. Tony Oliver, her senior engineer, would appear on the bridge to report her engines ready a matter of seconds before the captain rang down.

'Obey telegraphs!'

And they were ready this time. The admiral felt immensely relieved when he heard her familiar siren and saw her fall in astern of him. Force H set course for the Atlantic at twenty-five knots. When dawn came they were out of the Mediterranean, and at 5 a.m. the Swordfish of the first anti-submarine patrol began to come up on the lift like hunched, sleeping birds. As the day wore on the weather began to worsen, and landing-on became more and more hazardous.

At 8 a.m. came grave news. *Bismarck* had sunk the

Hood and badly damaged the *Prince of Wales.* All in Force H were stunned and shocked by this disaster, especially those who had served in the *Hood*, so recently their flagship. They steamed on in silence. The hours passed, with the seas increasing and the blue sky turning to grey.

Then another signal came in. *Victorious*, a hundred and twenty miles from the enemy, had launched nine Swordfish against her. One torpedo had hit *Bismarck* amidships. Was it the finish? Would they be sent back to Gibraltar?

Then reports of the enemy ceased. We had lost her.

Dawn came on 25th May and still all was silence. Where was she? Refuelling at this very moment from a tanker at sea, ready to fall upon our convoys? Was she heading for Brest, or the Straits, and a break through to join the Italians? Dare they think it: *was she heading this way*?

So everyone wondered and argued and worried aboard *Ark Royal* as she butted her way through huge green seas, heavy blinding rain, and howling winds.

The seas grew in size, the ran in force, the wind in velocity, making flying a fearful danger. Anxiously the engineers watched the pounding, over-worked engines. Speed was reduced to twenty-three, then twenty-one knots. Visibility grew worse and worse.

Still no reports. What chance of finding *Bismarck* now?

One thing they did know. She had not turned back. Aircraft from *Victorious* had searched the sea towards Greenland and found nothing.

Had she made for America, then, or . . . The other possibility was unthinkable. *The Straits were unguarded; the door was open.*

Then, just before dusk, *Bismarck*, which had fought so brilliantly and outwitted all her pursuers, blundered at last. She sent out a signal.

Instantly our direction-finding stations fastened upon it. We had a fix on her.

In *Ark Royal* the tension tautened, hearts beat faster. *Renown* altered course and speed. *Ark* followed. In the briefing-room the Swordfish pilots made calculations. The implication was plain.

Some time next morning they might be taking off to attack the greatest battleship in the world.

But their spirits sank as the day dragged on and the weather grew worse; so bad, in fact, that by the evening they were fighting a full gale. Clouds and heavy overcast hid the horizon. Would *Bismarck* elude them as she had done *Suffolk* and *Norfolk* at the onset of battle? Would they be able to get an aircraft into the air at all?

By dawn it did not seem likely. Captain Maund sent an officer to measure the rise and fall of the flight-deck.

'Fifty-three feet, sir,' he reported. It was unheard of, if it were accurate, to fly off an aircraft in such conditions. Maund sent a pilot to check the information. Gloomily he returned.

'First wave fifty-*six* feet, sir,' was his verdict.

It looked impossible. Even if he got off the deck no pilot could land on an eight-hundred-foot airstrip pitching fifty or sixty feet and rolling heavily.

At 8.30 a.m. ten Swordfish were brought up. They had to be held down on deck. Spray drenched the aircraft-handling party, and water swirled round their ankles. In five minutes it was time to fly off and look for the *Bismarck*.

The first machine rocked down the deck, wheels rolling through green water. Then the fifty-knot wind took it and flung it into the air – inches from the crest of a huge sea that smashed down across the bows.

'As the aircraft came forward and passed close below us on the bridge,' said Captain Maund, 'the observer or wireless gunner gave us a smile, read the last instruction about the wind on the blackboard, pushed his thumb upwards . . . and was off into the storm-swept sky.'

Time passed with no sign or sound of the enemy.

Then, at 10.50 a.m. came a signal. *Bismarck* had been glimpsed in the mist. She was fifty miles west of *Ark Royal*, somewhere beneath the Swordfish.

At 11.14 a.m. came, '*Bismarck* in sight!' from one of *Ark*'s planes.

This was it. Two Swordfish had got a fix on her. She could not be lost again.

From every point of the compass ships converged upon the raider. *King George V* and *Rodney* made all speed from the west, *Dorsetshire* from the south-west, Vian and four destroyers from the Home Fleet, while aircraft were brought to readiness all over southern England.

But the burden of striking the *Bismarck* first lay with the planes that came from the *Ark*. They must go in and cripple her. First, however, the reconnaissance force must return, land-on, and the striking force arm itself for the attack.

This was the batsman's finest hour. Braced upright at the side of the heaving deck, lashed with a lifeline, he somehow guided them all aboard. If he had misjudged by a second the exact moment at which to give the pilot the 'cut' it would have meant a plunge into the sea for the two airmen. The *Sheffield* was there astern, but snatching a man from that raging sea would have been a desperate business.

Meanwhile two more planes with long-range tanks had gone to take over the job of shadowing the enemy. For there were still two Swordfish in the air, holding *Bismarck* grimly through the gale. When these two returned their crew were rushed to the bridge. Then it was:

'Did you see *Prinz Eugen*?'

'No, only one ship.'

'What did she look like?'

'I think it was the *Bismarck*.'

'What about her silhouette? Was it like this one or more like this?'

'It was more like the *Prinz Eugen.*'

'Was there a gap between the funnel and the bridge?'

'No.'

'How big was she?'

The consensus of reports from the pilots described a ship more closely resembling *Prinz Eugen* than *Bismarck*. But they had peered at her through bad weather, when she was nothing but a low grey shadow on a grey, heaving sea. When they went close to check her identity her ack-ack fire drove them off.

Renown signalled, 'What is the report from the reconnaissance?'

Captain Maund replied, 'There is only one enemy ship. The evidence favours her being the *Prinz Eugen*, but I am sure she is the *Bismarck*.'

By 2 p.m. fourteen Swordfish waited in *Ark Royal*'s hangars for the weather to let them get at the *Bismarck*, *Ark* herself thrusting at full, and more than full, designed speed to close the gap, her gallant engines racing, her worn shafts driving her on through the gale.

Ten minutes later it was decided that the Swordfish must go – or lose the *Bismarck*. At 2.50 they struggled off the deck, formed up, and disappeared into the murk and heavy cloud.

They had just gone when an urgent signal was thrust into Captain Maund's hand.

Sheffield had been detached from Force H and was at this moment shadowing *Bismarck*; she was directly in the path of the aircraft from the *Ark*. They had not been able to tell *Bismarck* from *Prinz Eugen* an hour since. The weather was worse now and visibility even poorer. *Would they know* Sheffield *if they came upon her?*

'Look out for *Sheffield*!' the signal went out in plain language to the Swordfish.

It was too late. Eleven of the fourteen striking aircraft had loosed their torpedoes at the *Sheffield*. Luckily some were defective. These exploded prematurely. The cruiser avoided the remainder.

While the chagrined and frustrated striking force returned to the carrier and began to land-on, one of the shadowing aircraft waited patiently to do the same. At last its turn came. As the Swordfish approached she fired a Very light to warn the ship that she would have to make a crash landing. As she sank towards the stern, watchers on deck saw her propeller suddenly stop in mid air. Down she came in a falling leaf, side-slipping towards the rundown.

She missed it by ten yards and a great gasp of disappointment went up from those around the flight-deck. Then, before this huge sigh had faded, they saw the nose of the aircraft poke up over the roundown. Her swift fall had spun the propeller and squirted the last pint of petrol into the cylinders. The machine sprawled on to the flight-deck and missed all the arrester wires. The watchers held their breath once more. But as it coughed its way up the deck its hook caught the top strand of the wire barrier and slammed it to the deck.

Only faulty magnetic pistols in some of the torpedoes plus instant avoiding action by the *Sheffield* had averted a possible tragedy. It was a maddening, possibly calamitous fiasco. And now, with *Bismarck* in range, *Ark*'s sorely tried engines began to give trouble. All through the last three weeks the engines had been ranging continually from thirty knots to seven, as she alternately worked up to full speed for operating aircraft then rejoined the convoy and reduced again. They had had about as much of a caning as they could stand. Tony Oliver was in his cabin when the telephone rang. An agitated voice said,

'Senior, sir; the main circulator's on fire!'

The main circulator pumped all the cooling water through the main condenser. The bearings and thrust pads had 'run', the white metal had melted and two metal parts had rubbed together creating the flash which had set the lubricating oil on fire.

Oliver's first reaction was, 'Don't let it stop!' If the

156

machinery stopped now it meant the loss of one engine. He immediately had the fire main hose directed on to the thrust housing and buckets of olive oil poured continually over the white-hot parts. At the same time he put three really experienced engine-room artificers to keep a constant watch over the circulator.

As soon as they could be ranged and armed another striking force was flown off. With it went every Swordfish left in the ship. This time magnetic pistols were not fitted. Their torpedoes would only explode on impact; they had to *hit*.

Fifteen torpedo-bombers stood between *Bismarck* and safety. Now the greatest test of the Fleet Air Arm, of the carrier weapon, had come. *Ark Royal* had been created for this moment.

The aircraft picked up *Sheffield*, shadowing *Bismarck* doggedly, and from her obtained their course to steer for *Bismarck*. Everything rested with them. If they missed, or failed to slow the great vessel down, she would escape. The whole grim chase would be a terrible failure. The *Hood* would have gone to her martyrdom in vain.

They left the *Sheffield* and plunged into thick cloud. The foul grey miasma swirled about the frozen faces of the pilots and split the formation.

They came on the enemy in twos and threes or singly. The cloud and rain that obscured the target also hid the Swordfish from the lookouts on the *Bismarck*. But when the first machine appeared and came in low over the water a great bank of fire burst from *Bismarck*'s guns and hung along her side flashing and winking. Some of the planes were riddled with holes, but none was mortally hit.

Neither, as far as they could see, had they hit the enemy. They made for the *Ark* as soon as they had dropped their torpedoes, and it was not until they were back on board that a shadowing Swordfish signalled safely the results to Force H.

The news came at 11 p.m. The *Bismarck* was drifting

out of control. One of the torpedoes had hit her amidships, and another had wrecked her steering gear.

After that it was merely a matter of execution. During the night Vian's destroyers came up and attacked with torpedoes. On the following morning *King George V* and *Rodney* commenced firing.

She would not go down. Much to the satisfaction of the torpedo pilots the commander-in-chief was forced to signal,

'Cannot get her to sink with guns.'

Dorsetshire closed her, fired five torpedoes into her side, and she slowly rolled over and sank.

CHAPTER VIII

THE THIRTEENTH DAY

'At sea. Woke to find everything vibrating like the devil, with the ship doing twenty-four knots. We have *Renown* and *Sheffield* and five destroyers with us. Had a long talk from the Commander (Flying) with all the other pilots on deck procedure for flying off. In addition to the Skuas who are leading us, we are picking up a Sunderland flying-boat after about a hundred miles which will lead us the rest of the way. Had a run over my aircraft for R/T test, and ran over engine. Everything O.K.'

Thus a young Royal Air Force pilot, a temporary guest of *Ark Royal*, wrote in his diary on 2nd April 1941. The next morning he and his fellow passengers in their twelve Hurricanes took off, led by two of *Ark*'s Skuas, and headed for Malta.

These machines, and the twenty-three more which the *Ark* delivered at the end of the month, were worth their weight in gold to Malta. The little island had endured a savage mauling at the hands of the Luftwaffe in March, and her fighters had been reduced to a badly battered few. It was familiar work to the *Ark* by now, and something really worth doing, although the carrier's poor native pilots, contemplating their beaten-up Fulmars, hated to see those lovely Hurricanes go. . . . She and *Argus* kept up a regular transfusion service of Hurricanes to Malta, and resumed the work after Force H had returned from the *Bismarck* battle.

The situation in the Mediterranean had changed. The fight for Crete was in its very last throes, and the ships of the Mediterranean Fleet were bringing the last of our weary and wounded soldiers away from the island. By 1st June it was all over in Crete, and the Germans had sealed off the Balkans. Their southern line through Crete and the Dodecanese secure, they were now free to turn on Russia. They withdrew their bombers from Sicily, and sent them to the new front.

Compared with the terrible fighting of recent weeks, a summer lull now fell upon the Mediterranean. Now was the time to send all the aid we could to Malta, to give her more fighters to help bring in food and ammunition convoys, and above all, to build up her bomber strength and hack at Rommel's lifeline from Italy.

This was done. More Hurricanes were ferried in. *Ark Royal* and *Furious* between them delivered forty-seven on 21st May. On 15th June *Ark Royal* and *Victorious* delivered forty-seven more.

Some of the new Hurricanes were adapted as bombers. They joined the Wellingtons, Swordfish, and Blenheims which set about Axis ships bound for Libya and raided Naples and Tripoli and Sicilian airfields. Thanks to the *Ark*, the *Argus*, and the *Furious*, Malta was in business.

They worked out a standard routine and technique for the delivery of the Hurricanes. The *Furious* would bring them from Britain. This was always a happy occasion. *Furious* and the old *Argus* were both made honorary members of the Force H Club, and when *Furious* came in she was invariably greeted by the band of the *Ark* playing 'Ferryboat Serenade'. *Furious*'s own band replied with 'Colonel Bogey'. Captain Maund had a special ramp made to stretch from the flight-deck of the *Furious* across to *Ark Royal*'s roundown. The Hurricanes were then pushed along this bridge on to the *Ark*, and one or more of the three carriers sailed before first light and flew off the fighters to Malta in the vicinity of Cape Bon in Tunisia.

The much-increased number of Hurricanes now in Malta as a result of this delivery service made it possible to give fighter cover to convoys practically all the way from Gibraltar to their final anchorage in Grand Harbour, Valetta.

As a result, Operation Substance was mounted in late July to pass a big convoy through to Malta. It was to be a two-way operation. Six storeships and one troopship were to be sent to the island, and the fast auxiliary *Breconshire* and six other empty ships brought out.

The convoy started from Gibraltar on 21st July. *Nelson, Edinburgh, Manchester,* and *Arethusa* were lent from the Home Fleet for the operation. At the very outset the trooper, *Leinster,* ran aground, and had to be sent back to Gibraltar with five thousand troops and a contingent of R.A.F. mechanics on board bound for Malta. The rest of the force carried on, with the Mediterranean Fleet trailing its coat in the Eastern Mediterranean to draw the attention of the Italian Fleet from the convoy, and submarines patrolling the approaches to enemy harbours.

The German bombers had gone for the time being, but the Italian torpedo-bombers which attacked this convoy displayed a courage and tenacity well up to Luftwaffe standards. The attacks began early on 23rd July. The *Manchester* was badly hit by a torpedo and sent back to Gibraltar. The destroyer *Fearless* was so badly damaged that she had to be sunk by our own forces, and the *Firedrake* was torpedoed but managed to stay afloat. The attacks went on with unabated ferocity. *Ark Royal*'s outnumbered fighters and the anti-aircraft guns kept the force clear of further damage until the escorting force divided and Rear Admiral Syfret took charge of the convoy, bringing all six precious storeships safely into Grand Harbour on 24th July. Then he returned west to meet Somerville and head for Gibraltar. The whole force reached there safely on the 27th. The *Leinster* contingent was sent through on 2nd August in three cruisers and two destroyers. Meanwhile the Italians made a very daring attack on Grand Harbour and the recently arrived convoy with small craft, but the whole force was sunk by the Maltese coastal batteries and by some of the Hurricanes which Force H had previously brought.

Firedrake had been badly hit on her starboard side, and her whole boiler-room there exposed to the sea. *Ark Royal* escorted her back to Gibraltar. The morning after they had tied up Percy Hancock noticed a small boat, pulled by an elderly man dressed in dungarees and a white sweater, float into the gaping hole where the destroyer's boiler-room had once been. The quartermaster leaned over the side of *Firedrake* and shouted,

'Hey, you! What the —— do you think you're —— well doing?'

'It's all right,' said the oarsman, 'I only wanted to be the first man to row a boat round a destroyer's boiler-room.'

It was Admiral Somerville. They might have known. The admiral was really the heart of Force H. Whenever he could he came over to the *Ark* and flew in the back seat of a Fulmar or a Swordfish. He loved the kick it gave him, and the escape it afforded from the cares of being Flag Officer, Force H. He was also a leader who built his authority upon a close understanding of the young men who had to carry out his orders.

There were often amusing signals. When the news came in that Admiral Somerville had been given a second knighthood *Ark Royal* signalled,

'Fancy twice a knight, and at your age, too.'

Somerville's own famous signals often hid sharp stings. He well knew the difficulties of operating aircraft,

162

of course, but would never allow excuses. 'A delay in landing aircraft,' writes Maund, 'and a signal giving the reason why was expected before the question had even been asked by the flagship.' If *Ark* had trouble with the wind and had to turn about and steam in the opposite direction to the rest of Force H she could always expect this sort of thing:

'What are you looking for? A cat's paw?'

'No. It was for four knots of wind, which is the cat's whisker.'

'Alphabetical MEOW!'

On 24th September Operation Halberd, another convoy movement to Malta, was sent through; nine fifteen-knot ships this time, escorted by *Nelson, Rodney, Prince of Wales, Ark Royal,* five cruisers, and eighteen destroyers, carrying over two thousand troops as well as stores.

Just before *Ark Royal* sailed, her new port midships multiple pom-pom guns arrived on the dockside. Jack Bishop and his fellow ordnance men, working night and day, got them hoisted inboard and bolted down just in time. The addition was very welcome. They never found out whether the enemy knew that they had been operating for months without these guns, but most of the Italian torpedo-bombers seemed to attack from the port side. . . .

O'Nion, the air-gunner from 808, was a 'looker', with his Fulmar unserviceable, and on this trip he got an unusual view of the action. He saw the *Nelson* open up with her sixteen-inch guns at small dots in the distance, which were the Italian torpedo-bombers coming in almost at sea-level, sending up great spouts of water in the hope that the attackers would fly into them, a method which was sometimes successful.

This time two were shot down and two more sheered off. But two others were more persistent. They came straight in over *Nelson*'s bows and headed for *Ark*'s port side.

There had been no time to train a proper crew for the

new port-side pom-pom. It was manned now by a pilot and a few odd cooks and sweepers. Nor had there been time to join it up electrically to all the other gun-control circuits and directors.

The Italian bomber headed straight into the muzzles of the new guns, right into the faces of the gash-hands at the controls.

The bomber flew on. Still they did not fire. Standing by their side O'Nion could see every detail of the aircraft, and the torpedo slung underneath, which would be released any second now....

At that second the new gun burst into life. Its fire hit the torpedo, and the Italian disintegrated with a great flash.

The second bomber came on, following the track of the first. Fire from the pom-poms was hitting him, and bits were flying off the aircraft, but still he came on.

'When's he going to drop that tinfish?' was on everybody's lips.

Suddenly, about two hundred yards from the ship, he nosed over and crashed headlong into the sea. A great cheer went up from the *Ark*.

Then it was *Nelson*'s turn. She took a direct hit from a torpedo. She did not sink, but struggled on at convoy speed until nightfall, then turned and headed slowly back to Gibraltar. One merchant ship, the *Imperial Star*, was lost on the convoy, but the other eight ships arrived safely in Grand Harbour at 11.30 a.m. on 28th September.

Their arrival was well-timed, for now, at the end of September, the British Eighth Army in North Africa was being built up ready for a big attack on Rommel, and Malta was going to take a vital part in the offensive. Rommel and his mixed German and Italian army had already begun to suffer from the activities of Malta-based bombers and submarines standing between him and his source of supply. Now the Navy added to his plight by sending Captain Agnew to Malta with Force K, the cruisers *Aurora* and *Penelope* and two destroyers. It was the job of Force K to deal with any Italian convoys heading for North Africa which were too strong or too elusive for the Malta submarines or aircraft. On 8th November the force carried out its brief by annihilating a convoy of ten ships bound for Benghazi, and sinking two of its four escorting destroyers, another of which was sunk next morning by the submarine *Upholder*.

The Navy kept the Malta offensive going flat out by continuing the flow of fighters, fuel, and supplies into the island.

Force H went on ferrying Hurricanes. On Wednesday, 12th November, a young R.A.F. sergeant-pilot wrote in his diary:

Our first flight took off the *Argus* when the Blenheims turned up at 10.15 a.m. All took off O.K. except Pilot Officer L——. He had never flown a long-range Hurricane before. He swung violently to port. He nearly killed me and several others. His wing passed over W——, H——, B——, and me as he went off over the side a little higher up the deck. I just had time to think: 'Thank goodness I've got fat J. H—— in front of me.' I then looked forward and down expecting to see L—— in the sea; but he wasn't, he was flying, and his wheels were retracting, too.

As usual everybody who was free came up to watch the Hurricanes take off, standing around *Argus*'s catwalk. One of these was Sam Leigh. After he had left the *Ark Royal* the supply chief had visited her many times, for like all those who had gone to other ships he kept a permanent spot in his heart for the *Ark*. Hadn't he been with her at the very beginning, helping to fit her out and start her off well, to make her a fit floating home for her sailors and airmen? It was easy for him to slip ashore from the *Argus* in Gibraltar and come aboard his old *Ark* once more.

He watched the inexperienced Pilot Officer L——

break *Argus*'s flag and almost knock off his own tail wheel, then went below.

On the following day, 13th November, *Ark Royal*, *Argus*, *Malaya*, *Hermione*, and seven destroyers were returning to Gibraltar. The weather was fine, and men were loafing on deck, taking it easy after the strain of another ferrying trip.

All the *Ark*'s men felt themselves veterans now. There were many of her original ship's company still aboard, men like Jack Bishop, whose hard work for and at the guns had done so much to keep the old ship afloat in the face of all the heavy attacks she had had to face. Cyril Calder had seen hard service all the time as a leading seaman, and for some time had had the very responsible duty of leading the flight-deck party, without whose swift and expert work the *Ark* could never have operated her aircraft so well.

Percy Hancock was a chief petty officer telegraphist now, and as such had come much more closely in touch with the aircrews. He had never lost the wonderful glow of satisfaction he got every time his department successfully homed a lost aircraft to the ever-welcoming bosom of the *Ark*. John Coward, the chef, had had good reason to remember with a smile the words of that drafting commander at Pompey, back in '39: *I will call you in after twelve months as I notice you have had a good deal of sea time.* . . . Here he was, still in the *Ark*; and he'd had more days' sea time since then than the drafting commander had had hot dinners!

Many of the *Ark*'s old officers were gone. 'Big Bill' Eccles had left the ship, and she had seen two captains, both well loved and admired, come and go. New officers joining the ship, whose name really was a household word at home, very soon came to love her as much as their predecessors had done. Her senior engineer, Tony Oliver, had been with her now since before her Norwegian days, and had helped to make her the wonderful fighting ship she was. Pilots like 'Jimmy' Gardner and 'Winkle'

Esmonde, who had led the attack on *Bismarck* from *Victorious,* kept alive the thrusting, flashing spirit of those who had died over Trondheim, on the Malta convoys, and in the Atlantic.

All these men were happy in the *Ark*. She was for them as solid and secure as the Rock itself. Most of them who were off duty on this sunny day of 13th November lolled on deck or had their heads down below.

Over on the *Argus* Sam Leigh was keeping watch in the cipher office.

About a quarter to four in the afternoon he looked out across the shimmering water towards the *Ark Royal* and saw her suddenly heel over to starboard.

It was tea time on board. *Ark Royal* was thirty miles from Gibraltar and within sight of the Rock. She was landing-on aircraft, and the last machine was awaiting its turn to fly aboard.

The great shattering explosion found many men in the act of drinking their tea. Cyril Calder had his cup to his lips when the crash came. The cup was dashed out of his hand, and the mess table collapsed. . . . Claydon was sipping the hot, syrupy liquid when all the lights went out in the mess and the ship lurched and listed to starboard. . . . Jack Burnett had just had a shower ready to go on duty at six o'clock, and was having a cup of tea when the tremendous shock threw the mess into darkness. All the metal lockers toppled over with a crash. . . . Percy Hancock was buttering his bread and thinking 'I won't have any jam today, just plain bread and butter for a change. . . . '

O'Nion had been flying that afternoon, and had only just landed-on. He had gone to his mess, and was just picking up a cup of tea when the terrific explosion shook the whole ship. His tea went one way and he went another. A great flash came in through the hatchway. . . . Down below, in John Coward's mess, someone said, 'It's a depth-charge from one of the Swordfish. . . . ' They had in fact been hit amidships by a single torpedo fired from

U-81 or U-205, who had been hunting the *Ark* as a pair.

Everybody went swiftly to their action stations. Lieutenant-Commander Oliver had been sitting in his cabin when the explosion and violent shock came, looking at his stamp collection. He immediately rushed down to the machinery control-room. Already, he noticed, men were shutting the watertight doors all over the ship. When he got down to the control-room he could tell at once by the gauges that they had been hit in the starboard boiler-room.

'We've been hit, we've been hit . . .' men were saying everywhere, as if they could not believe that this had happened to the *Ark*.

Percy Hancock discovered that all power had failed, so that the ship's broadcasting system, and most of the telephones, were out of action. He reported to the captain that his orders would have to be passed by pipe.

Cyril Calder went to his action station below. Down there they thought it might be dive-bombers after them, but when the ship remained at an angle they knew it was a submarine.

O'Nion reached the flight-deck and saw that the ship was listing badly to starboard. A petty officer from his squadron shouted,

'Get the dinghies out of the aircraft in the hangar!'

O'Nion rushed down to the hangar where he found an officer and two ratings from the squadron going round from plane to plane pulling the quick-release wires which automatically set free and inflated the aircraft dinghies. But to their disgust they found that they could not get them through the access lobbies.

By this time the list had increased alarmingly. Captain Maund gave the order to abandon ship.

O'Nion went out on to the port weather-deck, where everyone was collecting. Some of the men had already jumped into the water, but the majority had waited as they could see the destroyer *Legion* trying to get alongside.

Lieutenant Gardner had thought for a second of going down to his cabin again to collect a few personal belongings, but decided against it now. Always in the back of his mind there had lurked the thought of the men in the *Courageous* who had returned below for that purpose just before she sank, and had been trapped there below when the lights went out, and they tried in vain to grope their way to safety through the dark, tilting passageways. . . .

The sea was rather choppy now, but the *Legion* made a perfect approach up the port side from astern. Soon men were swarming down ropes to her decks.

Someone had flung a rope down from flight-deck level right in front of where O'Nion was standing. As he went to grab it someone above him jumped on to it. The rope shot out of his hands and left him teetering on the deck edge. Just as he was about to fall the rope swayed back into his hands. If he had fallen he would have been crushed to death between the ship and the destroyer.

Many others went down the ropes. Others, like Claydon, jumped from the lower hangar-deck on to the *Legion*'s fo'c'sle.

John Coward found himself on the flight-deck. Captain Maund saw him standing there. 'Climb down that rope,' he said. Coward clutched the rope and shinned slowly down it. When he had gone down a few feet he looked down and found that the rope was much too short to reach the *Legion*.

'Jump, Shamfer!' shouted a man on the destroyer's deck. There was nothing else for it. He let go and landed with a crash on the heaving deck.

Before they left the ship those men who owned canaries brought them on deck and were to be seen opening the cages so that the little birds could fly away from the *Ark*. . . . Others saw to it that the cats which had been her pets were put into boxes which would float. In one of these was Oscar, who had been rescued from the *Bismarck*, and subsequently made welcome aboard the

169

ever-friendly *Ark*, and in another was a ginger cat which had once fallen off the flight-deck into Gibraltar harbour, climbed out on to the dockside, and walked calmly up the gangway on board the *Ark* again.

Captain Maund had decided that there was still a chance of saving the ship and with this in view kept on board those men who were immediately concerned with her safety.

Percy Hancock kept an operator on the emergency set in the port wireless office, and tied a piece of string with a weight on the end of the receiver to mark off the degree of list. The ship was gradually heeling more and more, and they could hear the sickening crash of aircraft and stores in the hangars as they rolled and crashed to starboard.

It was a weird, unnerving feeling, the ship so deathly quiet after being such a living, bustling thing, filled with the noise and clamour of men and machines.

In the engine and boiler-rooms they were fighting a desperate battle to save the *Ark*. After he had closed up in the machinery control-room the senior engineer had gone round inspecting the damage. Someone said they thought there was someone trapped in the starboard boiler-room, so Oliver went down there. He crawled in and found it flooded and in darkness. He called out, 'Is there anyone there?' but got no reply.

By now the centre boiler-room was beginning to flood rapidly as well. He reported to the captain, then returned below to organise all efforts to keep the ship afloat. Slipping quickly into his cabin for a moment, the first thing he noticed was a pencil hanging on a piece of string – stretched out stiffly at a wide angle from the side of his desk. He stared at the pencil, then pocketed the gold cigarette case given to him by his wife as a wedding present. Then he thought, 'No. That won't do at all!' and put it back.

The most serious damage was the loss of feed water. Because of this there was no power available anywhere to operate the pumps and vital machinery. To provide water and enough power for the pumps and some of the lights the destroyer *Laforey* came alongside. She cast off again when *Ark* managed to raise steam once more and get her dynamos and steering engine into action.

There now seemed to be some hope of keeping her afloat. At 7.30 p.m. a tug arrived and was soon pulling the *Ark* through the water at two knots. Down in the port boiler-room Oliver and a gang of volunteers were trying hard to get steam on the port shaft. Another tug arrived to help with the towing. *Ark*'s speed increased to five knots.

But her list was increasing all the time as well. Although Oliver and a number of volunteers had personally seen that all watertight hatches below were closed, the sea seemed to be filling the ship in spite of them, through that great wound in her side.

Soon the whole casing of the port boiler became red hot. The terrible heat and fumes began to overcome everyone down there.

Oliver and Chief-Stoker Walley came to the conclusion that the funnel uptakes must be under water. The senior engineer sent a man to report conditions to Captain Maund.

Eventually things in the boiler-room became unbearable. Two men fainted and Oliver was almost overcome. Everyone was ordered up.

Finally Oliver and the chief stoker remained. Oliver wanted to be the last to leave.

'If you try and wait till last you'll never make it,' said the Chief, and insisted that he go first up the ladder.

Almost unconscious, Oliver struggled desperately to reach Captain Maund. He found two men who supported him on either side and dragged him towards the bridge.

At last he could feel the wind on his burning face, and gulp the fresh sea air into his choking lungs. Near him he caught sight of the commander's immaculate, white-clad form. With a last desperate effort he thrust himself

171

forward and hung on to this tall, steady figure, such a citadel of strength and calm, with the world toppling all round. . . .

Ark was well over on her side now. Hancock and the other chief telegraphist tried to get over to the starboard office to salvage the scale-model railway which the latter had made for his son, but everything was toppling and crashing around them, and it was much too dangerous. Hancock went back and joined the captain on the port side of the flight-deck. They made a lonely group as they stood there in the darkness on a sinking ship.

In the distance they could see the lights of Gibraltar. In their hearts they knew that the *Ark* would never sail into harbour again.

'Let me know when the top of the funnel is level with the horizon on the starboard side,' said the captain quietly to Hancock.

Not long afterwards the funnel drew level with the dim line of the horizon. It was the end. They got ready to leave the *Ark*.

It was difficult to move about now. All the ladders were swinging vertically from their hinges, and heavy gear was breaking loose everywhere. Hancock reached the quarter-deck, rising from the water like a steep cliff, but could not jump clear because of the propellers. So in the darkness and silence he walked along the side of the wardroom until he was amidships. There he saw an M.T.B. waiting to take them off.

Eventually there were nineteen of them in the boat, and they stayed there and watched the *Ark* sink. She was alone on the sea for a while. It was dark and quiet, and they looked on silently, not trusting themselves to speak.

But in their hearts they were all saying the same thing. *Poor old girl, she does not want to go. She was a good ship to us right to the end.*

Presently a launch came out from Gibraltar with Admiral Somerville. He joined the others and watched the slow death of the *Ark*.

Captain Maund and Admiral Somerville were watching from the bridge of the *Laforey* when, at six o'clock in the morning, the *Ark* turned right over. The Admiral took Captain Maund below then, so that he would not have to witness her last plunge.

So she disappeared, and glided down through deeper and darker shades of light to the bottom of the sea. When she had finally gone her deck-hockey goalposts were left floating on the sea. . . .

One man went with her, an old able-seaman drowned when the rushing water engulfed him as he lay asleep below. *Ark* is asleep now, with him as her last custodian, a great, silent, haunted ship.

When her ship's company, sad and silent, were all assembled ashore in Gibraltar, they held a meeting to decide what should happen to the surplus canteen funds. It was decided unanimously that a silver bell should be purchased which could be put aboard the next ship to bear the name *Ark Royal*.

When the war was over and a new carrier with the proud old name had slid down the slipway and gone into service, many of the old ship's company came and presented the new vessel with the bell. It was a beautiful object, and it bore the inscription:

MAY THE SOUND OF THIS BELL REMIND US
OF THE POWER AND HARMONY OF MEN

THE END

PQ17 – CONVOY TO HELL

by Paul Lund and Harry Ludlam

In June, 1942, Convoy PQ17, consisting of thirty-five merchant ships, set out for Russia with an escort of cruisers and destroyers. They had a reasonable chance of success until the order came to 'Scatter!'

What followed represents one of the most terrible and tragic blunders of the Second World War.

Authors Ludlam and Lund give a first hand account of the horror and despair that faced the men left to the mercy of a cruel enemy. From thousands of sources and recollections they have built up an unforgettable picture of what it was like to be in PQ17 – and survive...

NEW ENGLISH LIBRARY

NEL BESTSELLERS

T011 682	ESCAPE ON VENUS	Edgar Rice Burroughs	40p
T013 537	WIZARD OF VENUS	Edgar Rice Burroughs	30p
T009 696	GLORY ROAD	Robert Heinlein	40p
T010 856	THE DAY AFTER TOMORROW	Robert Heinlein	30p
T016 900	STRANGER IN A STRANGE LAND	Robert Heinlein	75p
T011 844	DUNE	Frank Herbert	75p
T012 298	DUNE MESSIAH	Frank Herbert	40p
T015 211	THE GREEN BRAIN	Frank Herbert	30p

War

T013 367	DEVIL'S GUARD	Robert Elford	50p
T013 324	THE GOOD SHEPHERD	C. S. Forester	35p
T011 755	TRAWLERS GO TO WAR	Lund & Ludlam	40p
T015 505	THE LAST VOYAGE OF GRAF SPEE	Michael Powell	30p
T015 661	JACKALS OF THE REICH	Ronald Seth	30p
T012 263	FLEET WITHOUT A FRIEND	John Vader	30p

Western

T016 994	No. 1 EDGE – THE LONER	George G. Gilman	30p
T016 986	No. 2 EDGE – TEN THOUSAND DOLLARS AMERICAN	George G. Gilman	30p
T017 613	No. 3 EDGE – APACHE DEATH	George G. Gilman	30p
T017 001	No. 4 EDGE – KILLER'S BREED	George G. Gilman	30p
T016 536	No. 5 EDGE – BLOOD ON SILVER	George G. Gilman	30p
T017 621	No. 6 EDGE – THE BLUE, THE GREY AND THE RED	George G. Gilman	30p
T014 479	No. 7 EDGE – CALIFORNIA KILLING	George G. Gilman	30p
T015 254	No. 8 EDGE – SEVEN OUT OF HELL	George G. Gilman	30p
T015 475	No. 9 EDGE – BLOODY SUMMER	George G. Gilman	30p
T015 769	No. 10 EDGE – VENGEANCE IS BLACK	George G. Gilman	30p

General

T011 763	SEX MANNERS FOR MEN	Robert Chartham	30p
W002 531	SEX MANNERS FOR ADVANCED LOVERS	Robert Chartham	25p
W002 835	SEX AND THE OVER FORTIES	Robert Chartham	30p
T010 732	THE SENSUOUS COUPLE	Dr. 'C'	25p

Mad

S004 708	VIVA MAD!		30p
S004 676	MAD'S DON MARTIN COMES ON STRONG		30p
S004 816	MAD'S DAVE BERG LOOKS AT SICK WORLD		30p
S005 078	MADVERTISING		30p
S004 987	MAD SNAPPY ANSWERS TO STUPID QUESTIONS		30p

NEL P.O. BOX 11, FALMOUTH, TR10 9EN, CORNWALL
  Please send cheque or postal order. Allow 10p to cover postage and packing on one
book plus 4p for each additional book.

Name ....

Address...

   ....

Title ....
(SEPTEMBER)